ALL THE KING'S ORPHANS

LYNETTE CARPENTER

WestBow
PRESS*
A DIVISION OF THOMAS NELSON
& ZONDERVAN

WestBow Press books may be ordered through booksellers or by contacting:

WestBow Press
A Division of Thomas Nelson & Zondervan
1663 Liberty Drive
Bloomington, IN 47403
www.westbowpress.com
1 (866) 928-1240

ISBN: 978-1-5127-1633-7 (sc)
ISBN: 978-1-5127-1635-1 (hc)
ISBN: 978-1-5127-1634-4 (e)

Library of Congress Control Number: 2015916937

Print information available on the last page.

WestBow Press rev. date: 10/23/2015

CONTENTS

PREFACE
HADASSAH

She sits alone… cold…shivering.

Stretching her tiny frail arms around her knees, she pulls her legs up tightly to her chest, wishing to fight off the cold.

The loneliness.

The fear.

Peeking through a wayward strand of hair, Hadassah takes in the beauty of her surroundings. Gleaming marble stretched from beneath her out across the expanse of the grand entrance. Large wooden doors stood tall, displaying ornate beauty all their own. White columns circled the room, giving a sense of welcoming, security and strength.

"Tia." His voice calls out, warm…loving. "Come, My princess. Come join us."

Hadassah's heart trembles with desire. How she longs to rise from her cold loneliness and join the others. But she…she can't. She just… she just can't.

Hoping He'll understand, Hadassah turns away quickly lest he see the tears gathering so quickly in her eyes.

His invitation comes often and she knows it will come again. Does He not see? Does He not know? Does He not understand her dilemma?

Moments pass before she finds the courage to look once again into the room where He sits. Around Him, children giggle and play. Some sing, some dance, while others drape themselves over the armrest of His chair watching the glow of the warm fire dance across His face. He entertains them with stories and words of comfort bringing much laughter and joy.

Hadassah's sorrow is soon replaced with annoyance. Who do those kids think they are? Why do they get so much time with Papa? Why must she sit here all alone while they laugh together in the warmth of the living room?

Soon, it is time for bed. Papa rises from His chair. The children hug Him tightly before scurrying off to their rooms amid shouts of "good-nights" and "I love yous". A few stop by and rest a hand on Hadassah's shoulder, "Good night, Tia. Sleep good." Hadassah only nodded, her head still turned away.

Papa came near and knelt beside her. The warmth from His presence drew Hadassah in, but she knew she couldn't crumble. Couldn't let her guard down. There was too much at stake. Too much to lose.

"Tia, love. What's troubling you?"

Tears fill Hadassah's eyes so she buries her head deeper, wishing He would sweep her up into His powerful arms... yet at the same time hoping He'll go away.

"I'm fine, Sir."

"You don't seem fine, Tia." Papa settles in beside Hadassah, leaning His back against the wall near the place where she sits.

Silence fills the room with only the occasional crackle from the fireplace, the sound of doors closing upstairs and children's voices murmuring quietly as they prepare for bed.

"Tia," His voice quieter still. "How long will you sit here? How long will you hold Me at arms length?"

Burning tears settle in behind Hadassah's eyes as the pain of emotion claws heavily at her throat. Shaking her head, she shifts ever so slightly, turning her back on Papa.

He notices, but is not swayed. "When I found you... out there... alone and miserable on the streets, I brought you here because... because I want so much more for you. So much more than the life you were living." He pauses for a moment and then, "Don't you want that too?"

Hadassah nods, her face still buried in her pencil-thin arms.

"Then come with Me! Let Me show you all the things I have for you."

Hadassah lifts her eyes to meet Papa's, searching… questioning… wondering. Uncertainty blends with hope and desperation. Could He really give her more than this life she had always known? Could there really be beauty and hope and joy?

Papa stands to His feet and reaches for her hands. Standing slowly, Hadassah stretches out and takes His.

Papa smiles and Hadassah sees the pleasure in His eyes. He truly loves her, truly cares. She can sense it. Can feel it.

"Come this way," He says, "I want to show you the room I have prepared for you." Papa turns toward the stairway and Hadassah allows her eyes to drift across the expansive foyer towards the grand staircase. The marble floors reach the base where they are met by dark mahogany steps. The stairs curve around, wide and welcoming, as they climb their way to the second floor.

Hadassah takes one step and then stops. Papa pauses as well, and looks back, a question on His face. "What's the matter, My Tia?"

"Just wait, Sir, I… I need to get my things." Hadassah drops His hand and begins gathering her belongings. Hurrying, she places her knapsack on top of a small box and carries it to the stairs. Setting it down, she rushes back across the foyer and gathers up two more boxes.

Papa stands watching as Hadassah makes several trips and then finally, uses her little body to push one last larger box to the base of the stairs.

"Tia, honey," Papa starts and then stops. They've had this conversation before. Just yesterday, when He'd first brought her to His home, Papa had told her she could leave the boxes. "Tia," He'd said, "You won't need to bring anything. I have all that you need. You can leave all your baggage behind."

Hadassah appreciated the offer, but Papa... He just couldn't understand. She *needed* these boxes. They were all she had left! They were hers! Lord knows, she had precious little in this world, and she wasn't about to give up the few things she had... no matter how much Papa had to offer.

Papa's eyes fill with sorrow but He reaches for her hand yet again. "Come, I'll show you your room first, then you can come back for your boxes."

Hadassah hesitates, but then, content with the decision, follows Papa up the stairs.

CHAPTER 1
ADOPTED

It's been a while ago now. I don't remember where I was or what I was doing. I simply remember the vision... or was it a dream?

Either way, the story has stuck with me. It's the story you just read. The story of an orphan child being taken in to the home of a King. I saw her there, so alone. Filled with sorrow. Desperate to be loved...yet reluctant to accept it.

When my vision came to an end, Jesus spoke to me, "This is a picture of My church. My bride. Many have come into My Kingdom, yet are unwilling to shed their past and accept all that I have for them. They find themselves living in a Kingdom but refusing the title that comes with being the child of a King. I have given them a new name, yet they see themselves still as orphans - unable and unwilling to fully accept the freedom, joy and beauty of Kingdom living."

I have pondered this many times, and while I cannot claim to fully understand all that this means, I am beginning to see a picture of the Western church in the vision of the little orphan who refused to be called by a new name – Princess.

You see, Hadassah still lives inside those palace walls. She has full rights as a princess, yet in her mind, she is still an orphan. She still sees herself as alone, unloved, not belonging and without the security of a father.

Where can she be found? This Orphan Spirit can be found teaching Sunday School, singing in the choir and sitting next to you in the pew.

And maybe…just maybe, you might see one everyday when you look in the mirror.

***

I was born with red hair. This, accompanied by my abundance of freckles, set me apart from my brown haired, freckle-free siblings… and, it gave my brother all the material he needed to convince me that I didn't belong.

"You're adopted. That's why you have red hair. Mom and Dad found you on the doorstep."

He was teasing, of course. Just fulfilling his brotherly role of messing with his little sister. But what he told me made sense.

I *was* different! The more I thought about it, the more his words solidified in my mind pointing out all the differences between myself and the rest of my family – even conjuring up some differences he had not yet identified.

I was the *only* red head.

I didn't look *anything* like my parents.

Besides that – he and I are less than a year apart in age. No humans with any kind of common sense would willingly choose to have two children so close in age.

The doorstep story seemed like a stretch, but it did leave lingering question in my mind. Did I belong?

I wasn't very old before I learned that my situation was not that unique. There are many siblings who have parents as crazy as mine – parents who ended up with two babies in less than a year.

And yes, I was the lone redhead in the family, but that fact alone didn't determine my bloodline. Not knowing my thought process, my grandma once pointed out that my nose was just like hers – "flat and pudgy". Um... thanks. Ok... I guess I fit in after all.

My questions as a child are a reflection of the thoughts of many people in the world today.

Why am I different?

Where do I belong?

How did I get in this situation?

What is my purpose?

Who am I?

I have many friends who are adopted and their stories inspire me. Though some struggle with those questions of identity, they have a distinction that I, and the rest of us living with our biological families do not possess – *they* were chosen.

That is the beauty of adoption. When a man and a woman, of their own free will, make the life-changing decision to give a child a family.

A home.

Security.

Provision.

An identity.

Love.

Recently, some friends of ours went halfway around the world. They had a mission. They planned, saved, prayed, cried and rejoiced when they got the news. Far away, in another country, in a city most knew nothing about, was a tiny orphanage with one special little girl.

Out of all the children there, they chose her.

This child was abandoned and had been living in an orphanage since she was a baby. Her birth family was unknown and even her age was debatable.

In spite of the fact that she carried a disease, didn't speak a word of English and had nothing to offer them, Jon and Carissa still wanted her. They claimed her as their own, gave her a name and a place to call home.

That day, a little girl we'd never met became co-heirs with a houseful of siblings and she now enjoys equal rights to all her parents have to offer.

Now consider this - I've known Jon and Carissa far longer than this sweet child from Uganda has. I knew them before they were married. I knew them before they had kids. I listened to them speak of their hopes and dreams to one day adopt… I have been to their house – even watched as they built it. In spite of how much I know about my friends, it doesn't make me their daughter, therefore, I do not have the same rights this one little girl from the other side of the world now enjoys.

In their home, Eva's rights exceed mine.

She can wander freely throughout their home, dig in the pantry, open the refrigerator, and help herself to the good things her mommy and daddy have for her… something you and I would not have the right to do in their home.

Eva's adoption is an illustration of what we as God's children experience when He takes us into His kingdom. Millions of people claim to know God… and many know a lot about Him – but just knowing about Him doesn't make you His child. To become His own, we must go through the process of being adopted into His family.

Adoption is mentioned numerous times throughout the Bible. Let's take a look at several of those stories.

The first adoption we read about is seen in the life of Moses. (If you aren't familiar with is story, you can find it in Exodus 2.)

Moses was born to parents who loved and cared for him, yet through a series of events, he ends up being adopted by the princess of Egypt. As we know, Moses went on to lead the Israelites out of slavery and is remembered as a great hero of the Bible.

But have you ever wondered what God was thinking when He allowed Moses to be taken from his parents and moved to the home of the enemy? I know I have!

From our place in history, we have the privilege of looking back at Moses' story and seeing how beautifully God orchestrated his life, yet you can't help but wonder how Moses felt about being adopted. Did he see his family from time to time? Was he jealous of Aaron and Miriam - wishing he could have been raised in their family home? Why couldn't Moses have stayed in the home of his biological family and still become the man God needed him to be?

We can look at the terrible atrocities brought on when Pharaoh killed the Israelites babies – because it was terrible…but God was able to use that horrible experience to move Moses to a strategic position in order to gain something he wouldn't have been able to attain had he been raised in the home of slaves. God longed to set His people free from the bondage of slavery and to do that He needed to prepare someone for a specific position of leadership. It couldn't be someone from among them - the Israelites had been slaves so long, they no longer knew how to think and act like free men.

They had a slave mentality.

They were so accustomed to their bondage, they didn't know how to live without it. For so many years they didn't have to think for themselves. They ate what they were told to eat, did the work they were told to do, lived where they were told to live, slept when they were allowed to sleep…the list goes on and on.

Leaving Egypt meant leaving all they knew. Suddenly the world lay before them with an overwhelming amount of options… and it was scary! So at the first sign of discomfort or distress in the free world, we see the Israelites begin complaining… wanting to go back to Egypt…willing to go back to their bondage.

God couldn't have a leader with that mindset. He couldn't have Moses grow up with a slave mentality. He needed someone who was free. Someone who knew how to walk with confidence. A person who knew who he was and that his name held authority.

It needed to be someone who had been taught in the ways of royalty.

Another Bible story about adoption is about a boy named Mephibosheth.

Mephibosheth was actually born into royalty. He was the son of Jonathan, King Saul's son. Mephibosheth's early life was one of prestige, wealth and ease, but his grandpa, King Saul, was a wicked man. One day, God had enough.

When Mephibosheth was only five years old, King Saul was killed on the battlefield and the kingdom was overthrown. In the chaos of trying to escape, Mephibosheth was hurt and crippled for life.

Not much else is told about him other than that he is taken to a place called Lo Debar where he lives for many years. What's interesting is that Lo Debar means a place of 'no pasture'.

It was a place of desolation. Not only that, Mephibosheth's name means Son of Shame. Talk about a depressing life!

In the meantime, back at the palace, King David had taken over the throne and began his reign. Years went by and David started wondering about his old friend, Jonathan. He and Jonathan had been exceptionally close friends and the king asked if any of Jonathan's family was still alive.

This led to Mephibosheth being found in Lo Debar and whisked off to the palace. Imagine the fear that must have been coursing through his veins! What did the king want with him? He arrived before King David, well aware of his position. He was a cripple - in that culture, this alone made him an outcast. Worse yet, he was the grandson of the king's greatest enemy – this was certain to be the last day of Mephibosheth's life!

Imagine his surprise when King David began telling of all that he was giving to Mephibosheth! He returned all of Saul's land to the young man! Mephibosheth would no longer have to live in Lo Debar – he would no longer have to live in desolation.

But the king wasn't done. King David chose that day to take Mephibosheth in as one of his own. He wanted to give him a home and a place at his table!

As Believers, we, too, have been adopted. God, the Father, has chosen us, though outcast, broken and living in desolation. It matters not to God what our social status is, how great our belongings, how pristine our family history - nor what we have to offer Him. He simply desires to have us *with* Him – to call us *His* child.

Just as David gave Mephibosheth a place at his table, we too have been offered a place at the King's table. God longs to give us a name. He desires to give us security and love and the ability to walk through life knowing who we are and Whose we are.

He did this through the death and resurrection of His Son, Jesus Christ.

Galatians 4:3-7 (NLT) says,

> *"...Before Christ came. We were like children; we were*
> *slaves to the basic spiritual principles of this world.*
> *But when the right time came, God sent His Son,*
> *born of a woman, subject to the law.*
> *God sent Him to buy freedom for us who were slaves to the*
> *law, so that He could adopt us as His very own children.*
> *And because we are His children, God has sent the Spirit of His*
> *Son into our hearts, prompting us to call out, "Abba, Father."*
> *Now you are no longer a slave but God's own child. And*
> *since you are His child, God has made you His heir.*

How exciting!

An heir to the Kingdom of God?

Have you ever stopped to consider, *really* consider what that means? If this is true, the Kingdom should be filled to the brim with royal offspring having the time of their lives!

Romans 8 tells how the children of God get to fearlessly enjoy adventure after adventure as we live within the security of His Kingdom. With child-like expectancy, we can call out, "What's next, Papa?" knowing He brings all things together for our good.

Somehow this doesn't sound like the Christianity we see in the current western church though. Am I right?

Why is this?

What's the problem?

I believe the issue is that though adopted; too many are living within the walls of the Palace still clinging to their former identity.

An identity that refuses to allow them the freedom of a peace-filled, fearless Kingdom experience. An identity that tells them they don't belong, they don't fit in, they're not good enough, they're all alone and that God the Father cannot be trusted.

It's an identity known as the Orphan Spirit.

This spirit is plaguing the churches of North America. It's stealing our joy, promoting fear, and is a catalyst for division.

To understand the Orphan Spirit, we must also understand the orphan and his mindset.

The orphan is lonely, unable to trust, desperate and afraid. His life experiences tell him he can only afford to watch out for himself. He preys on the weak, is uncomfortable -unless he's in control, he manipulates situations to fit his agenda and loathes seeing another get something he wanted. His existence is self-focused, independent and self-entitled – but it's the only life he knows.

Sound familiar?

Consider this – what might it look like to live, really live, as sons and daughters of the King? Is it possible to move beyond the orphan mentality?

The following chapters are fictional characters experiencing real life struggles. You may be able to relate to them in various ways. The purpose of each story is to hopefully open our eyes to what we've been missing as Christians and to help identify various manifestations of the Orphan Spirit within the walls of the Kingdom.

Do we have to continue living a powerless, defeated, self-centered Christianity? No!

Let's learn together how we can shed our Orphan Spirit and, instead, discover the ways of royalty.

CHAPTER 2
THE SPIRIT OF JEALOUSY

Dana Reese checked her hair one last time in the mirror. Nice. She liked this cut.

"Good call on the curls, Reese."

"What, mommy?"

Ella's voice from the car seat reminded Dana that she was not alone.

"Nothing, sweetie. Mommy was just talking to herself." Another glance in the mirror, and Dana was ready to roll. She wrinkled her nose at her reflection, grabbed the door handle and got out.

Dana heard her best friend, Becca, pull up beside her just as she released Ella from her car seat.

"Hey girl!" Becca's voice was filled with joy and a warmth spread over Dana's soul. She always enjoyed spending time with her tall, annoyingly slender friend. Well, almost always.

Becca was sweet to a fault. Oh sure, she had her flaws, but sometimes they seemed much too few and far between.

"Hi Becca! How's it going?"

"Hi Dana," Becca's smile looked tired. "It's, well, it's been a morning, but...hey, you know, it's all good." Becca reached up and pressed a button on the ceiling and Dana watched as both doors on Becca's mini-van glided open without effort.

"Hi Aunt Dana! Hi Emma!" The voices of Becca's three and five-year-old daughters called out from inside the van.

"Hey Taylor! Hi Jessie! Are you excited to come play with Emma?" The girls nodded excitedly and Dana couldn't help but admire their matching sundresses and sandals. She let her eyes sweep over Emma's outfit and was relieved to see she was equally adorable, although she wished now she had chosen the new outfit she'd found at Target instead of the lady bug shirt and shorts her daughter now wore.

Oh well. It couldn't be helped. They were here now. She made a mental note to learn the new braid technique she'd seen on Pinterest last night. Emma would look adorable with that hairstyle.

Dana stroked Emma's long strands of caramel curls, inwardly thankful that her daughter didn't have the misfortune of short, thin hair like Becca's did.

Becca pressed yet another button and the back door of the van lifted. Taylor and Jessie grabbed Emma's hand and began walking towards the church. Dana tugged at her blouse, readjusted her purse and turned to follow the girls. Becca followed behind, holding a crate filled with who knows what.

"Did you need me to carry anything?" Dana asked.

"No, it's fine. If I need my purse, I'll come back for it."

Dana reached out to open the door of the church for Becca. "Thank you!" Becca smiled again as she sailed by.

Dana saw what looked like a pile of boards sticking out of the crate. "Whatcha got there, Bec? Another one of your crazy projects?"

"Yeah," There was a lilt in Becca's voice as she spoke with excitement. "Jeff had a bunch of pallet wood laying around the shop and I thought, 'wouldn't it be fun to make little signs for the women coming to mom's group?'" Becca set the crate on the nearest table inside their small fellowship hall and continued, "It was super simple. I just sanded them down a little and," Becca stopped and began rummaging through the crate, "ta-da!" Dana pulled out a beautiful, hand painted sign – *'Precious In His Sight'*. The décor was shabby chic and Dana knew the women would love it.

Dana didn't know what else to say, so she went the safe route, "Aww.."

"Here's another," Becca beamed as she spread the signs across the table, "I think it's my favorite, *'beautifully & wonderfully made'*. Isn't that a great reminder for mom's dealing with post baby bodies and all?"

"Oh yes." Dana knew her voice didn't match the excitement in Becca's. "I'm sure they'll like them."

"Which one do you want?" Becca's question took Dana by surprise.

"Oh, umm..." Dana looked over the collection of signs, and her eye immediately fell on one. The words curved delicately across the rough wood, *'WELCOME FRIENDS'*. Dana could imagine it resting on the table near the front door. It would be perfect there.

She hoped her smile reached her eyes as she reached out and picked the sign up from the table. "I'll take this one. So pretty. Thanks Becca."

If Becca had noticed Dana's lack of enthusiasm, she didn't let on. "Wanna get these tablecloths on? Was thinking maybe we could use the signs to decorate the tables."

Dana turned away, "Sure. Let me first go check on the girls." Dana didn't hurry and by the time she returned, Becca had put tablecloths on the table, added some flowers and placed a sign at each chair. Already women had started arriving and the gasps of delight and flood of compliments gushing from their mouths made Dana want to puke.

"Dana! Did you see these?" Erika came rushing towards her, her hands clutching an adorable sign with the words *'WAKE UP, GET DRESSED, BE AWESOME'* scrawled across the front. Why hadn't she seen that one earlier? That one was so much more fun than the one she had chosen.

Dana plastered a smile across her face, "Yeah, aren't they so sweet? I saw some like that on Pinterest." She raised her voice, and called across the crowd to Becca, "Did you find those on my Pinterest page, Becca? Love how super cheap and easy it is to make something like that." Without waiting for an answer from Becca, Dana tipped her head towards Erika and lowered her voice, "I'm planning to make some too… but I prefer a square sign over these rectangles. I mean, these are nice, but as soon as life slows down a little, I'd love to make a few of my own. Except… like I said… I'll make mine square."

Erika stared at Dana for a second as though unsure what to say, then looking back at the sign in her hand, she smiled and returned to her seat. Becca wove her way through the group of women, smiling and nodding along as they chatted happily about preschools, recipes, married life and, of course, the signs. Those dumb signs.

"What's wrong with you," she asked herself. *"It's just some stupid little signs. Who cares if she thought of it before you did."* Dana watched a group of women crowd in around Becca listening intently as she told some apparently hilarious story about spilling paint while making the signs.

"Give me a break." Dana inwardly rolled her eyes, yet couldn't help wondering why she even cared.

But Dana did care.

She cared that Becca always seemed to be a step ahead of her.

Every. Single. Time!

Becca was the one who had thought of bringing gifts today.

She was the one with the long, slender legs.

The one with the fancy-schmancy mini-van.

The one with a husband who offered to help paint those silly signs for these silly women!

She was also the one with adorably dressed children. Children who looked like they'd just been yanked out from a Pottery Barn catalog!

She was now the one with the crowd of adoring friends hanging on her every word!

She was so… so…*so annoying*!

Dana glanced at her watch. It was a little early, but she didn't care. Clapping her hands, she called the room to order. It was time to get started.

But deep inside she knew.

She knew that more than getting the meeting started on time, she just wanted everyone to stop going gaa gaa over those….those… those *stupid* signs!

Have you ever been there?

Living in the shadow of that one friend who seems to strike gold no matter what they do?

The fact of the matter is that it's not so much about the good fortune the Beccas in our lives seem to have – it's more about the attitude we have towards them.

You see, Dana has an Orphan Spirit. Her spirit manifests itself predominantly through jealousy. Dana is a child of God, living in the Kingdom, yet she has not yet taken on His name. She doesn't see herself as one who fully belongs and her thought process tells her she has never been good enough.

The Jealous Orphan Spirit struggles to celebrate the good fortunes of another. They are much like the one child at every birthday party who complains that they didn't get a present. Dana could have chosen to celebrate her friend – after all, she called Becca her best friend, yet even in that, she was unable to bring herself to point out Becca's good qualities.

When Becca arrived at the church that morning, Dana had overlooked the fact that Becca sounded discouraged. All she could think about was everything that Becca had in comparison to herself. She compared children, vehicles, outfits, and more. In her mind, Dana was keeping score. She valued their friendship… but only so long as she was in the lead.

The further ahead Becca became (in Dana's mind), the more distance Dana put between them until she actually found herself belittling her best friend to other women in the church.

The Jealous Orphan Spirit hates when another is given special treatment or attention. She operates out of insecurity and struggles to promote others. She finds joy in minimizing another's talents while searching for ways to maximize her own.

Her struggles are born out of a need for identity in the family of God. As children, we grow up knowing who we are and where we belong in our family – whether good or bad. The Orphan Spirit is unsettled – never truly knowing who they are in Christ, if they are accepted and if they really belong.

They want to belong. Want it desperately, but life on the streets has robbed her of the gift of security. She will struggle to see others as brothers and sisters instead of rivals. And in that struggle, she will fail to understand that the promotion of another or the blessings in another's life are not a sign of God loving that person more and loving her less. On the contrary! Our Papa God delights in giving good gifts and His gifts in your life should stand as a reminder to me that He is a good and gracious Giver.

Imagine the difference in Dana's morning had she chosen to meet women at the door, signs in hand and praising her friend's generous heart and amazing talent. "Look what Becca did!" She could have said. "Isn't she awesome?!" "I think she did a wonderful job!"

Had Dana done that, her sisters in the church would have been drawn to her, Dana. Her love, acceptance and promotion of another would have communicated that Dana was a safe place to fall and she would likely have found her relationship tank overflowing. Instead, her jealous nature brings her to a place where she ends up criticizing Becca's gift, which in turn, isolates Dana from the others.

Does God promote people from time to time? Absolutely! He does grant special blessings in individual's lives during various seasons – and that's a good thing. Dana needs to realize that just because Becca has some of what she wants today, she, Dana, isn't less valuable in the Kingdom. God doesn't love her any less!

And maybe, just maybe, when she stops worrying about the blessings Becca has in her corner, Dana will be able to go see the ones her Abba Father has placed in hers.

Because you are precious in My eyes,
and honored, and I love you,
I give men in return for you,
peoples in exchange for your life.
Everyone who is called by My name,
whom I created for My glory,
whom I formed and made.
Isaiah 43:4,7 ESV

CHAPTER 3
THE SPIRIT OF POVERTY

Keith and Carrie Jo Baker were running late…again.

Keith hated the stares coming from his fellow church members as their family of seven pushed their way into their pew.

"Cut it out," he pulled on Jacob's ear. Trying to get that boy to behave was like pulling hen's teeth. Jacob squirmed and pulled away. Keith caught a whiff of Jacob's shirt and shook his head. Didn't the kid change this morning. Come to think of it, seems like he'd seen those clothes on him all weekend.

Oh well.

The Davidsons were looking back, apparently disturbed by the unruly entry. Keith nodded and smiled their direction. Bob Davidson nodded back and turned back as the worship leader invited everyone to stand.

Keith noticed Carrie Jo looking Sarah Davidson up and down and wondered what was bothering his wife this time. He'd heard her complain about the snooty Mrs. D plenty of times to imagine the thoughts running through her head.

"She always looks at me like I'm trash… Just because they're rich, they think they're better than we are…" On and on the complaints would come. Keith knew Carrie Jo was right. The Davidson's were stuck up.

True, they'd actually offered to help the Baker's out from time to time. There was the time they'd needed a new carburetor and the Davidsons had offered to fix it for them, free of charge, in the mechanic shop they owned across town.

Keith doubted that Bob was even pulling in six figures but they obviously made more money than he did – why else would they have helped them out like that?

Keith snorted. Carrie Jo shot him a glare and he told himself to straighten up. Who was he kidding? It wasn't hard to make more money than him. Few people had worse luck than he did. He worked hard, but, somehow, it seemed things never worked out for him.

For example, there was the job at the used car lot in Salem he'd had last summer. He'd missed a few days here and there while his mom was in the hospital with kidney stones. Boss Man didn't seem to think that was a good enough reason and told him to find another job.

Thankfully, he'd bumped into Dave Hescher that same evening. Dave was an old buddy from high school and was looking for someone to make deliveries for his catering business.

Keith jumped at the opportunity; thankful Carrie Jo wouldn't have to worry even more about their financial situation.

He'd been working for Hescher Catering less than a month when Dave called him into his office.

He wasn't happy with Keith's customer service. Apparently someone had called in and complained. Dave didn't say who it was, but Keith had a feeling it was Donna over at the law firm.

Seriously?

Dave told him he'd give him another chance but Keith couldn't work under that kind of pressure. If Dave wasn't willing to stick up for him – his own friend, then Keith knew he couldn't trust him.

Keith stood to his feet, threw out a, "some kind of friend you are", and stomped out the door.

Carrie Jo was disappointed but agreed that Dave had been too hard on him. The following weeks had been difficult. With no money in their savings, Keith had filed for unemployment.

Again, the Davidsons had learned of their plight and Sarah D had slipped Carrie Jo a crisp $50 dollar bill after services one morning. The money was welcome, but with five children to feed, Keith couldn't help but wish they'd offered a Benjamin or two instead.

The song ended and Keith pulled himself back to the present. "Whatever you're facing. Whatever you're going through right now, you can lay it at the feet of Jesus. He knows your story. He knows your worries and fears." The worship leader paused as the music played in the background. "This morning, I invite you to surrender it all to Him. Let Him carry your burdens. Come… come and surrender it all."

Keith watched at the praise team flowed into an old familiar hymn.

All to Jesus, I surrender

All to Him, I freely give

I will ever love and trust Him

In His presence, daily live.

I surrender all

I surrender all

The song continued but Keith got stuck on that phrase… I surrender all.. "I would, if I could, Jesus. But I've got nothin' to surrender!"

Keith's thought slipped back to his current job situation. He'd gotten a job as a janitor soon after leaving Hescher Catering, but the hours were too early for him and if there was one thing Keith needed, it was his sleep.

He quit after five days.

Keith found odd jobs around town to keep them afloat while waiting for…what, he wasn't sure. The church had taken up a special offering for a family in need and he was grateful they hadn't mentioned who the recipients of that special offering would be. The money helped them make it through another month.

Around that time though, the local pizza parlor was looking for a delivery driver. Keith was stunned at the amount of people who had had the gall to suggest he apply. Were they serious? That was a job for college kids! He was a full-grown man, father of five! He even had his associate's degree! No, he would not be applying for some silly pizza delivery job, thank you very much! He was overqualified – that was the problem!

If things couldn't get worse around that time, Carrie Jo got hurt. The flooring in the living room had rotted out. Carrie Jo had sank through the sub-floor one night, breaking her ankle and leaving her laid up on the couch for a while.

Soon, a daily entourage of mini-vans and soccer moms were dropping by with casseroles and well-wishes. Keith hated the look of disgust on their faces each time they'd step their spotless Nikes inside the door of their doublewide. He knew his home needed some work. He'd get to it when he had time….and money. They weren't rolling in the dough right now…obviously!

After the first meal was delivered, he'd found a piece of plywood in the backyard and threw it over the hole in the living room floor. Shoving the round rattan chair on top of it, he nodded in satisfaction over his ability to disguise his quick fix.

That would have to do for now. Maybe if one of these hoity-toity ladies would have one of their husbands offer him a job, he'd actually have the money to repair the hole correctly. "Dream on, Baker," he muttered under his breath.

He kicked a pile of clothes into the corner and sat down. He knew it wouldn't hurt to have the kids help clean up the place, but he hated to pull them away from the PS4 they'd gotten for

Christmas. They'd get to cleaning up eventually…when things got better.

The meals had only lasted for the first week. The kids were bummed when it stopped and Keith couldn't help but feel bitter that the church wasn't providing more with Carrie Jo being on the outs.

Bitter didn't get the work done, so Keith became both Dad and Mr. Mom for a while. By the time Carrie Jo was back on her feet, he was glad to escape the confines of their tiny home and got back to looking for a job.

Turning his eyes toward the ceiling, he wondered if God even knew their plight. Did He listen? Was He aware of how bad things were? Pastor was always preaching about God being faithful… God being a provider… God caring about our needs. If that was true, Keith wondered, why God wasn't doing any of that for him?

***

"You create the environment around you that you carry within you."

I heard these words for the first time while listening to a Kris Vallotton podcast. The concept was a new and interesting one for me, and it came back to my mind as I researched the various aspects of the Orphan Spirit.

Part of an orphan's mentality is that there is never enough – they have a Spirit of Poverty. They are always in want, yet at the same time, are content to live in less than pleasant conditions.

Accustomed to handouts, they struggle to move into the mindset of royalty and embrace all that the Father has made available to them.

"But Keith's having a rough time," you say.

Really?

Let's talk about it. Keith has been given opportunity after opportunity to care for the needs of his family, yet he refuses to do his work with excellence and contentment.

Sons and daughters take on a sense of ownership and pride in their family and it shows by their willingness to sacrifice time, energy and comfort for the good of the family.

Since orphans do not have a sense of belonging, theirs is a tendency to blame others for their current circumstances. They struggle to trust others and, in so doing, cannot move into a relationship of equality. Instead, the orphan sees himself as a pauper and his lifestyle is a testament to that belief system.

Sons and daughters know who they are in Christ. Like Joseph in the Bible, they have the ability to turn their prison into a palace. They are able to reign even in the worst of situations because their surroundings reflect what they hold inside.

Does this mean you should never have a messy house or go on welfare?

If that's your question, you've missed the point.

Of course you can have those situations in life. The freedom comes when there is a change of belief about who you are as a child of God.

When you see yourself as one who has a position in the Kingdom… one who has been fully accepted…adopted and given a new name, you stop looking to others to meet your needs… and you also stop blaming them when they don't. You find yourself willing to do what God calls you to do in order to care for your family.

Keith's focus remained solely on self and the failures of others. The only time he focused on God was to blame Him for not meeting *his* needs. Truth is, God had provided multiple jobs for Keith. Keith just didn't care to make the effort to keep them. He found fault after fault after fault with each opportunity that was presented to him.

Can I propose that maybe it's time to stop focusing on the negatives and start focusing on the positives?

I know of a man who made a conscious decision one day to look for the good in every situation. He realized that it was so easy to get caught up in a negative mindset and he determined he was going to change.

And change he did. I found that his positivity was contagious. When talking to him, I too, began searching for uplifting things to point out about people as opposed to bringing up their faults.

He then took it upon himself to spread the joy. Ask anyone who runs into him on any given day, and I guarantee they'll tell you how this man gave them a reason to smile. At the beginning of 2015, many began making New Year's resolutions, and once again, this gentleman made a commitment that startled me – yet shouldn't have.

His 2015 resolution is to "tip more".

That's right – tip more. He plans to give higher tips at restaurants and the like... and boy, has he! There are times his wife is taken aback by the amount he leaves on the table, but because she trusts him with their finances (and deeply admires his generosity), she says little.

I happen to be that wife.

My husband, Tim, is an illustration of a son who trusts in his Abba Father. Tim lives his life openhanded. He knows that God is able to give *and* to take away. But even with the "take away" possibility out there, Tim trusts his Father. Truth is, Tim and I have experienced the giving and the taking away. We've had years of plenty and years of just scraping by, but God has been the same God in both situations. He is good – and can be trusted!

My husband knows that God will work all things together for our good...and because of that, Tim is able to freely give – with joy – to so many.

Our Abba Daddy truly is a provider. He's a good provider. Sometimes His provisions aren't what we would necessarily expect, or even want, but I believe He is calling His children to experience deeper levels of trust in Him as their Father.

He has not called us to live with the Spirit of Poverty. We are no longer orphans! It's time for the body of Christ to take their rightful place in the Kingdom. It's time to start *trusting* in our

Father and know that He is ready and waiting. He longs to see us leave the poverty mentality and finally surrender all.

> *This resurrection life you received from*
> *God is not a timid, grave-tending life.*
> *It's adventurously expectant,*
> *greeting God with a childlike*
> *"What's next, Papa?"*
> Romans 8:15 MES

CHAPTER 4
THE SPIRIT OF FEAR

The feeling was back.

Cold, nagging fear. It clawed at her neck, wrapping itself around her throat and spreading down to the depths of her being.

The fear, it was so familiar to her. She couldn't imagine life without it. And though accustomed to her miserable companion, Valerie couldn't help but long for a moment without it.

What would it be like to feel laughter in her soul? To let her smile meet her eyes? To sleep in heavenly peace?

What would it feel like to breathe deeply?

Valerie let the hot suds of the dishwater bring warmth to her fingertips.

She was cold. Always cold.

A by-product of her frigid soul? She didn't know, but, perhaps.

A quick glance at the clock and Valerie knew she had wasted enough time. She gave a quick swish of the water and watched it drain away. Time was short, but Valerie never left the sink without giving it a thorough scrubbing. If there was one thing she wasn't, it was unkempt.

Her friends often teased her for taking too much pride in the care of her home, but Valerie knew it wasn't pride. It was more than that. So much more.

Somehow her girlfriends just couldn't understand that the neat-as-a-pin home was her calm in the storm. Her last ditch effort to mask the chaos in her heart. Life may be out of control, but at least her home was within her tightly-held, well-manicured grasp. The organization gave her peace. Brought tranquility...serenity.

Calling for the kids to come, she let out a groan. "No, no, no! Why didn't you listen to mama? Go change into the clothes that I laid out for you!" Jesse and Ellie turned and ran back to their rooms, knowing better than to cross their mother.

Valerie glanced at the clock and breathed a quick sigh of relief. She still had time to call Janie. She toyed with the words in her head, trying to find the exact way to present her idea. She didn't want to hurt Janie's feelings, but really, she had a job to do. She was the kitchen lady after all! The Pastor had entrusted this ministry to her care and no one would stand in her way in providing good, quality, wholesome food for the members of her church. The thought of disappointing the leadership made Valerie close her eyes and shudder. She was perfectly capable. And she would prove it!

Besides, what was Janie thinking? Her home was filled with cats – everyone knew that. Valerie hated cats and the thought of cat dander touching her food was enough to churn her already tied-in-knots stomach. Who knew what all had went into that spaghetti Janie had brought to the last fellowship meal!

Valerie's heart raced a little faster as she listened to the phone ringing in her ear.

Once.

Twice.

Five times and finally switched to voicemail.

Yes! Thank You, sweet Jesus!

"Hi, Janie?" Valerie kept her voice light and airy, "I was wondering if I could get you to do me a favor? We are needing two bags of shredded lettuce for our next fellowship meal and...well, I just love how I know I can count on you for anything. Sooo..." Valerie noticed Jesse and Ellie coming out of their bedrooms and shot them a 'you-better-be-quiet glance'.

They were.

Valerie continued, her voice still sweet and full of energy, "I was wondering if you would be so kind as to volunteer to bring those this Sunday? Of course, if you bring that, I absolutely wouldn't want you going to the trouble of bringing an additional dish to pass. Hope that works for you! Thanks, and have a wonderful day!"

Valerie clicked end and tossed the phone in her purse. "Let's go, kids." The drive into town was blessedly quiet.

Jesse and Ellie donned headphones and watched a DVD in the back. Valerie hoped it was the educational DVDs she had recently purchased but was too tired to check. Her thoughts were already draining away her energy.

On the radio, the song ended and the familiar jingle announcing the news began to play. The cold fear she'd felt while washing dishes returned. Colder still. Should she listen?

Valerie hated the news. Hated the crime, the chaos, the politics, the wars, the stock market. She hated it all!

Why couldn't there ever be good news?

The solemn voice on the airwaves confirmed her belief and began filling her in on the latest epidemic sweeping the nation.

The fear clawed at her again – her chest this time and she squirmed in its weighty grasp. What should she do? What if they caught this latest virus? What were the symptoms? Should she skip going to the store?

But she needed milk. And bread. And she really wanted to stock up on bottled water in case a greater emergency hit. And maybe some extra candles. And, for heaven's sake, why hadn't Bob purchased that generator yet? Didn't he know how crazy this world was?

The worries piled up on top of one another as Valerie pulled into the parking lot of the local grocery store – her mind racing with horrible scenarios of all the what-ifs in life. As quickly as the fears would come, she grasped for solutions, desperate for some peace of mind.

But every option left her feeling desperate, alone, helpless and abandoned.

The kids climbed out of the van and walked silently beside her. They were used to this version of mommy. One wrong move would result in severe punishment. It wasn't worth crossing her path.

***

Something had happened to Valerie.

Oh, she thought she was over it. Everyone did. And maybe, in some ways, she was. But the night her daddy left had changed her. He had been her rock. Her hero. Her knight in shining armor.

He had been the one who tucked her in at night and the one who made her giggle with his silly, fishy faces at the dinner table.

But then he was gone.

Gone!

How could he leave without so much as a goodbye? She couldn't understand. The grief, it chased her. Chased her still.

In high school, she'd given her broken heart to Jesus. How thankful she was that He had loved her enough to die a terrible death on the cross. Valerie determined to spend her life proving her love to Him.

But she remembered. Oh, she remembered.

Remembered the loneliness, the questions, the hurting... the pain. She remembered the nights lying in her bed, wondering why she wasn't enough to make him stay. Asking God to make her beautiful enough to bring daddy back. Begging for an answer to a question – longing to know why he'd left.

Her answers never came and Valerie had to learn to live without a daddy. The wound she received from his departure began to heal, but not without scarring her terribly.

The orphan spirit must deal with abandonment and with it comes a Spirit of Fear. The orphan remembers life on the streets, learning to fend for herself. Even now the voice in her head taunts her, reminding her that she is not enough. Never enough. After all, she wasn't reason enough to stay – not even for the man who was supposed to love her more than life itself...the man who was supposed to walk her down the aisle...the man she'd called Daddy.

After having children of her own, Valerie's pain only intensified. Now she knew the fierce love that came with holding your newborn in your arms. She had been that to her daddy – but... still...he left.

Her pain produces a sad irony in her life in that her very own friends pull away, hurt by her controlling behaviors. Her children obey out of fear, unable to realize much of mommy's anger stems from constant battle with fear of her own – a fear of losing them. Even her husband will struggle to understand how to help his wife and knows he must tow the line in order to keep her happy.

The Orphan's Spirit of Fear leaves her holding tightly to all that she has, refusing to let go. It matters not if the things she holds are possessions, anger or a grudge. She trusts no one and prefers when control is placed squarely in the palm of her hands. Fear is her constant companion and her thoughts are totally focused on herself and her survival.

The Spirit of Fear is one of the most prevalent ways the Orphan Spirit manifests itself in the Western Church today. We see it in when religion causes us to love one another with an agenda - do what I want you to do and I'll love you. Don't do what I want you to do and I'll use guilt and anger in an attempt to manipulate you to return to my good graces.

Prime example? Gay marriage. How much of the outrage and disgust comes from a genuine love for the homosexual?

None!

There is no love in that! Is homosexuality a sin? Yes it is. So is fornication...and gluttony...and gossip... but those don't get the same amount of condemnation and judgment from the pews.

Why?

The reasons are various but I believe that overall a fear of God's judgment is the driving force behind the reaction of many when it comes to the subject of gay marriage. And, yes, the wrath of God is something to be feared and respected! Yet, I'm left to wonder what would happen if we were willing to stop worrying about how this might affect *us*, and start reflecting the love of Jesus to the outcasts and sinners of our society. Remember, the only place Jesus displayed anger and disgust was in relation to the religious – not the sinners.

It also should cause us to stop and consider why we are willing to overlook the sins in our own lives while throwing rocks at those who sin differently.

Another byproduct of the Spirit of Fear found within the Orphan is a tendency to hoard. It could be food; it could be money, or clothes... or even time. She uses the material things of this world to build up walls around her so she feels most safe and secure. She is self-reliant – never trusting that her Abba Daddy *wants* to provide these things for her, as she needs them.

Once she realizes her security in the Kingdom, a daughter of Christ is open handed. She cherishes the gifts God gives her, and she *utilizes* them. She knows He gave them to be *used* for her own pleasure as well as to bring joy to His heart when He sees her giving and receiving the good things He's provided for her.

While still living with the spirit of an orphan, Valerie will be unsure of her identity in the family of God. Since her earthly father broke her trust, she battles knowing where her place is in the Kingdom. She fears her vulnerabilities, inabilities and weaknesses will be exposed and she works frantically to stay covered and protected on all sides. She must be perfect in order to keep her Father God from abandoning her as well.

Oftentimes, the fear-filled orphan finds comfort in belittling others. The possibility of a brother or sister excelling over them is terrifying and they will do anything in their power to keep this from happening. Because of her constant fear of failure, she is one who needs constant reassurance from those in leadership over her life, and since she feels an inner lack of confidence, she feels an insatiable desire to prove herself to those around her.

When given a leadership position, the fear-filled orphan spirit becomes protective and territorial. She believes no one can do her job as perfectly as she. Handing over the reins is not an option and she is willing to do all that she can to keep that from happening.

Valerie used lies and flattery in her effort to manipulate an unsuspecting Janie when it came to the kitchen ministry. A few bags of lettuce may seem like a small thing – and in some ways it is, but often times, the orphan spirit will do what she must in order to retain control in her area of ministry.

If she has to lie, she'll lie.

If she has to cheat, she'll cheat.

If some gets hurt by her actions, too bad.

Survival is the goal, and the Orphan Spirit sees no other option for living.

To stand by and watch the Fear-filled orphan is tiring. Even more so, to be the one trapped within its restraints. The Orphan Spirit is a tireless lifestyle for the one who has not yet encountered the security and love of a Father.

I am reminded of the time when our daughter Amy was two. Our baby, Corey, was only six weeks old when I noticed Amy sprawled out in front of the stairs leading to the lower floor of our split level home.

She stayed there for what seemed like hours. In the busyness of mommy life, I didn't stop to consider why she was laying there, but eventually she began to cry. Her words were not easy for me to understand, but I finally figured it out – she was afraid Corey, who was laying on a blanket on the living room floor (two rooms away) was going to fall down the stairs.

No amount of convincing could get her to leave her post. "Amy, he can't walk – or crawl. Or even roll over! He's not going anywhere!"

She remained unconvinced. It wasn't until I took a chair, tipped it on its side and pushed it in front of the steps that Amy's fears were pacified.

Her fear was unfounded. From my perspective, I knew the chair was unnecessary for Corey's well-being, but to her, it provided comfort.

God spoke to me about her actions. "You do the same thing, Lynette. I have so many things for you to go and enjoy in My Kingdom, but you're unwilling or unable to move because of your fears. Do you know how many of your fears are unfounded? To you, they're huge possibilities, but to Me – they're as unrealistic as a six-week-old baby being able to move himself across a house in order to fall down a set of stairs."

And He was right! How much living – *really living*, do we miss out on because we let fear control us? We tell God to take us where He wants us, yet the unknown sends us running back to what we know…and what *we* can control.

Sons and daughters have nothing to fear, already safe in their Father's love and place in the family. They can trust in Abba's faithfulness no matter what comes their way. Once adopted, the child of God is secure in knowing that He is a Father that never leaves. He never fails. His plans may not always be evident…may not always make sense, but Kingdom kids are ever aware that He is working all things together for their good.

Those who have taken His name can live life free, at peace, and full of joy. They know that their lives are in His hands. They are confident in His love and live open-handed, ready to give and receive.

The fearless child of God can live with reckless obedience to the Father because they know that His love for them is endless and He can be trusted. Life takes on new meaning when sons and daughters decide to live lives as laid down lovers of God; completely surrendered to His will with total trust that He is good, His resources are limitless, and a love that points to Him rather than back to themselves.

Are not two sparrows sold for a penny?
And not one of them will fall to the ground
apart from your Father.
But even the hairs of your head
are all numbered.
Fear not, therefore;
you are of more value than many sparrows.
Matthew 10:29-31 NIV

CHAPTER 5
THE SPIRIT OF NARCISSISM

The music died down, only the pulsating beat of the drums and the drone of the piano chords hung in the air. Danny could feel the anticipation… the energy. This was his favorite part of the song. His turn to let loose and play with all his might.

He loved the response from the audience as he used his abilities to help lead them into worship. How could he describe the feeling he got when he played? It was addictive. Powerful. It was his drug of choice.

His *new* drug of choice, that is. So much better than the addiction that once held him captive.

Danny thought back to the days when getting high was all he could think about. He'd been homeless, sleeping on his brother's couch when it happened.

Shawn and his wife, Stephanie, were heavily involved in some Holy Roller church and they'd warned Danny that their small group was coming over that evening. Danny didn't much care for hypocrites… er… Christians, but he had nowhere else to go, so he took a shower, pulled a rumpled t-shirt from behind the driver's seat of his car (hoping it didn't smell too bad) and found a corner of the living room to hang out for the night.

The crew starting showing up around 6pm and soon the house was filled with the sounds of laughter and delightful smells of some cheese dip Stephanie's friend, Beth, had brought.

The tantalizing aroma was too much for Danny's empty stomach, so eventually he made his way through the crowd of Jesus freaks. If he had to put up with the crazies, he may as well eat their food to make it worth one night of misery.

He had just settled back in his corner again when some guy plopped down beside him with his own plate of food, a handshake, "the name's Darren", and a "how's it going?"

By the time the night was over, Danny's head was spinning. How had he ended up with these people?

He lay on the couch that night reliving the events. After eating with Darren, he reluctantly joined into a, mostly hilarious, game of Pictionary. Much to his surprise, and, perhaps, consternation, Danny found himself having fun.

Weird.

Eventually the laughter faded away and Danny found himself listening as yet another guy, Pete, picked up his guitar and led the group seamlessly into a time of worship.

Danny wished he could escape, but from his place on the couch, he felt trapped. Oh well, it wouldn't kill him to sit there, he conceded. Few knew his passion for music and he couldn't help but feel a stirring in his soul as he let the notes swirl around him.

That night had been a turning point.

Danny hadn't expected to have fun.

Or to even like these people.

And to be liked back!

That, in and of itself, felt not unlike the miracle of the bread and fish he'd heard about as a kid.

These people liked him! And it seemed genuine too!

Danny lay thinking later that night. Why were they all so nice to him? They knew nothing about him, so they couldn't be trying to buddy up to him for any selfish reasons.

Danny snorted. As if he had anything to offer them!

He had nothing! No home. No money. No life! Just an old beater he used to get him around – and even that was only on its best days.

Danny couldn't put a finger on it, but later that week when Shawn invited him to join him at Worship Practice, Danny caved.

The praise band hadn't yet arrived when they walked onto the stage. Introductions were made and Danny recognized a few faces from the previous night. "Hi Pete, hey Beth, yeah, yeah, good to see you too."

Danny was admiring the drum set when it happened. Shawn began talking about how "awesome" Danny was on the guitar and before he knew it, he found himself holding a beautiful electric guitar with a flat black finish.

It was sick!

He loved it!

Loved the feel of the strings under his fingers, the tone that filled the room and even the weight of the strap across his shoulder.

He closed his eyes and let his fingers find their familiar resting place on the frets and then... he tore it up.

'Thunderstruck' flew from his heart to his hands and out to his stunned audience of a dozen people. He knew it wasn't a churchy song, but he didn't care. From the looks on the worship band's faces, they didn't seem to care either.

Shouts of amazement and high fives followed his rendition of the ACDC song. The admiration felt good. Felt real good.

How long had it been since he'd done something to gain anyone's approval? Years? Ever?

Danny couldn't remember. It had been way too long.

Even as a kid, he'd failed to please his father. Shawn had always been the good son. The one to produce perfect report cards, sports awards and a gleam in their father's eyes.

If only he'd been so lucky.

No, he'd seldom felt the approval and acceptance of his father, and here, now, feeling the admiration of so many. Ok, well, maybe ten people, it felt... it felt wonderful. His lonely heart drank it up like a thirsty dog on a hot day.

That evening had been another night of change for him. Danny sat with Pete as the praise band cleaned up the stage at the end of the night and Pete asked him if he'd ever considered having a relationship with Jesus.

Danny didn't know what all that entailed, but if it meant hanging around these awesome people... if it meant having more of the happiness he'd experienced here and the night at Shawn's house, then yes, he wanted it! He wanted to get rid of the life he'd been living and make a change.

Pete led him through something he called a Sinner's Prayer. After they said 'Amen', Pete clapped Danny on the back and asked him if he felt different.

Danny didn't feel a whole lot different. Hungrier maybe, but he doubted that was the response Pete wanted.

"Yeah, man," he said. "I feel so much happier."

Pete smiled, "that's awesome, bud. Now, you need to start getting into the Word and praying – you know, just talking to God."

"Yeah. Yeah, ok."

"And here's my number, ok. You can call or text anytime, man."

Danny shoved Pete's number into his pocket and the two went to share the good news with Shawn.

***

The following months felt like a whole new world had opened to Danny – and in a way, it had.

He was warmly welcomed both into the church and, to his delight, the praise band. Danny had never felt more loved, more complete, more alive than when he stepped onto that stage each Sunday and picked up the borrowed guitar.

Even better were the compliments poured out on him after each service. Sometimes even throughout the week on Twitter and Facebook.

This Christian thing wasn't so bad after all!

But, the realities of life will always find you – and find him they did.

"Son, we need to talk."

"Hey dad, how's it going?"

"Good, son. Going good."

"What's up?"

"Your mother and I... we're worried about you."

"Worried? Dad, I've never been better!"

"Yeah, I see that. And I'm happy for you. I truly mean that. But your church life has nothing to do with what I want to talk to you about."

"Mmmmmkay, so... then what?"

"Well, we think you need to find a place to live. And you really need to get a job. Have you been looking?"

Danny's answer was mumbled and accompanied by a shrug. Why was it any of his dad's business? He was twenty-seven years old, for crying out loud!

Danny listened as Dad went on to talk about wanting to see Danny get a steady income, stable home and most importantly, *off* his brother's couch.

So that's what this was about.

Dad assured him that it was not, but it was too late. Danny had gotten the point.

Pete could see Danny's frustration at church that night and tried to encourage him. Danny appreciated his efforts, but the foul mood brought on by his father's advice got the best of him and he took it out on Pete.

He hated himself for the hurt he saw on Pete's face as he walked away, but, really, it was obvious he, himself was hurting. If Pete was the good Christian he claimed to be, wouldn't he come back and encourage him? Maybe invite him out for coffee? Better yet, offer him a job?

Danny made it through the rest of the week, and now, here he was, back to doing what he loved most. Hunching over, he played his guitar with all that he was. Sweat beads formed on his brow, a testimony to the energy pouring from his body.

His solo ended and Danny listened to the familiar cheers from the audience. Why were they quieter than usual? They were quieter, right? He allowed his gaze to sweep over the people. A few smiled back, but most were looking elsewhere, or had their eyes closed - lost in worship.

Hmm...

Danny tried to shrug it off but he couldn't deny that it bugged him.

He finished out the set and then scooted out the back as soon as he could get away. Pastor Dave was just beginning his sermon but Danny didn't care. He needed to leave. Needed to clear his head.

Danny reached his car and looked back, expecting to see Pete or Shawn or someone… anyone coming after him. But there was no one there.

Christians! Really? That's what they called themselves? Where was everyone when he was so obviously hurting?

The only answer he got was an empty parking lot and church doors that remained closed.

Hesitating only a moment longer, Danny climbed in his car and drove away.

***

Danny is struggling with an issue all too familiar inside the walls of the American church.

Narcissism. The dictionary describes narcissism as extreme selfishness, with a grandiose view of one's own talents and a craving for admiration. The word is synonymous with vanity, self-love, self-admiration, conceit and self-centeredness.

Our Western culture is saturated with narcissists and it has woven its way into the Kingdom. We are created to love and be loved, yet those living with a Spirit of Narcissism find themselves worn out by the same turmoil Danny faces.

Danny craves affirmation. He cannot rest in the knowledge and confidence that he is perfectly loved and adored by his Creator. Instead, Danny depends on others to fill that void in his life.

The constant need for affirmation is draining on those around him. Think about it. Does Danny know anything about Pete's life? What he's going through? What he's facing?

See, what Danny doesn't realize is that Pete's mother was just diagnosed with cancer. Yeah, he heard it mentioned during prayer time, but did he know...*really know* what Pete was going through?

Did he even care?

Honestly, no. Danny doesn't care. Sure, he wants his friend to be happy, but he's more concerned with Pete being who he, Danny, needs Pete to be *for him*. His encourager... supporter... cheerleader...friend.

Danny depends on the approval of those around him to keep him going and his greatest fear is that the love will stop. While he drinks in the attention, love and support, he also fights it off. He *needs* his brothers and sisters in Christ to *prove* that they'll love him no matter what.

Orphans are accustomed to disappointment. They do not know the love of a father or mother, so when taken in by adoption, there is a struggle to believe that this is for real. That this is a love that will last.

Wielding a sword, as it were, they jab at any brother or sister who tries to come close and then judge them for backing away.

Sons and daughters recognize that once adopted, they have a permanent place in the Kingdom. They have a position and are perfectly adored by their Abba Daddy…the Father who will never abandon them.

The Spirit of Narcissism thinks less of his relationship with his Father and more about his position among the siblings. He is reliant on their respect and adoration, and fails to understand when he doesn't feel as though he is loved and belongs. He sees the strengths of others as a threat and is unable and unwilling to promote others. Instead, he will seek to hide his own limitations as he continues to depend on others' response to him as a way to gauge his worth.

Sons and daughters accept both their strengths and weaknesses—comfortable with who they are and Whose they are. They *cover each other's weaknesses* – seeking to protect the family and to serve one another with joy. In that, they remember that their Abba

Daddy is the one who is worthy of all praise. And, somehow, there's relief in that.

Why?

Because, He is altogether perfect. Though we fail, He does not. As His child, He invites us to a place of unconditional acceptance and rest in our unique, God-given identity.

His desire to take us in and call us His own has nothing to do with who we are or what we've done or will do. It is simply because of His great love and compassion towards us.

And that is perfectly beautiful… and very much enough.

Not to us,
O Lord,
not to us,
but to Your name give glory,
for the sake of Your steadfast love
and Your faithfulness!
Psalm 115:1 ESV

CHAPTER 6
SPIRIT OF CONTROL

Was it the sunlight that awoke her, or, perhaps was the buzzing of a housefly dancing around her nose? Shay twitched her head in an unsuccessful attempt to chase it away. She blinked and slowly opened her eyes. The couch beneath her was comfortable enough – as long as she could ignore the coarse fibers of the upholstery pressing crisscross lines into the bruise on her cheek.

The fly returned, landing on her lip. Shay blew out a puff of air and it moved to her forehead. Annoyed, she reached up to flick it away. The simple movement took her breath away and she gasped in surprise at the intense pain along her rib cage. Tears flooded her eyes as memories from the night before filled her senses. She could still hear the cries of her little girl through the bathroom door.

Shay had knelt outside the door, clawing at the wood until her nails bled, begging Brett to stop. Offering him anything… anything he wanted if he'd only open the door.

Finally, there was quiet.

The door opened. Brett stepped over her as he dropped their whimpering daughter into her lap. Shay scrambled up and pulled the bathroom door shut behind her and Faith – locking Brett out. Clutching her daughter close, Shay collapsed to the floor where tears streamed down both their faces as they clung to one another.

Hours later, after she had laid a sleeping little girl in her crib, she tiptoed out to the living room – hoping to sleep on the couch. But he was there. Waiting.

The beating lasted longer than most and Shay wondered if she'd live to see the light of morning.

Now with a dull ache throbbing between her ears and the sickening taste of blood in her mouth, Shay eased slowly into a sitting position. Baby James whimpered beside her and she wondered how he had gotten there. Brett must have brought him to her before he left last night. She shook her head, angry at his apparent kindness after such insane abuse.

"I don't understand you, Brett Anderson!" A lump filled her throat, expanding until her ears hurt and a searing pain burned deep in the core of her spine. Raking her fingers through her hair, Shay spat the words towards Brett's empty chair, "I do not understand you!" Her words were low and guttural and they grated on her ears.

***

Brett slid the chair back from his desk and tossed a pile of papers onto an already full basket. His eyebrows furrowed, frustrated by the disarray around him, he punched a button on his desk phone

54

and called his secretary in. A moment passed before Melanie stepped inside the door.

"I'd like these papers filed." His words held authority. Melanie nodded as she rushed to begin filing said papers. Brett watched her work, admiring her trim figure and the way her hair fell around her neck and he softened.

"So how's Zack doing? I haven't seen him around for a while."

Melanie's face lit up, her love for her son was evident. "He's doing great. Busy with football at school." Her brow furrowed momentarily.

"Is something wrong?"

"No...well... sort of. His dad wants him to move to Missouri for the summer with him and his new wife." Melanie stopped as tears filled her eyes. "The whole thing... it just makes me sick."

"Hey... now... don't cry," Brett stood, walked over to Melanie and pulled her into a comforting hug. Melanie leaned her head into his shoulder, her words muffled against his shirtsleeve. Brett couldn't make out all that she was saying, but he continued to hold her close and offer words of comfort, "I'm sure it's not easy – trying to parent alone, but don't be so hard on yourself. You're such a great mom."

Melanie nodded and pulled away. Grabbing a tissue, she gently dabbed at the tears on her face. "I'm sorry. I've just been such a mess lately."

"Don't be sorry! You have a lot on your plate. You just need to promise me that you'll let me know if there's anything I can do to help." Brett could still smell her perfume on his shirt. He liked it. Liked it a lot.

Melanie nodded and turned towards the door, "Oh! I almost forgot! There was a call for you from your pastor this morning."

Melanie's words interrupted Brett's train of thought. Brett's face flushed as his heart skipped a beat.

"Am I supposed to call him?" Brett picked up the note, then just as quickly saw Melanie's words scrawled across the paper – "Elder's meeting tonight. 6:30."

"Nope," Melanie smiled, "Just a reminder about a meeting you have tonight."

"That's right! Thanks Mel! You're a lifesaver!" He flashed his most charming grin and settled back down at his desk. The elders were needing to connect real quick tonight right before prayer meeting. He'd forgotten. There was no need to feel guilty – he and Melanie hadn't done anything wrong. He was simply concerned over the welfare of his employee.

A little hug was completely appropriate – perhaps even expected. He was after all, a Christian, and Christians were supposed to show love to those around him…and that was exactly what he had done.

Setting the reminder note aside, Brett entered the Elder's Meeting into his online calendar. Fewer things had given him more satisfaction than being called up to sit on the Elder Board of the church. He and Shay were still young – barely thirty, but his leadership skills couldn't be hidden. It was Pastor Mike who had first approached him. Brett still remembered the conversation.

"Brett," Pastor Mike had said, "We deeply admire your work ethic, your willingness to serve and the way you lead your family. We need more men like you in our congregation."

Brett had felt his chest swell with pride as the pastor's words fell on his ears. He was right! Brett did work hard! Very hard! And he had a lot to show for it too.

Brett's eyes fell on the framed photo of his family on his windowsill. The kids were beautiful and healthy. His wife, caring and… well, she had that extra weight. Seemed like she hadn't been able to shed it between pregnancies. Baby James was only a week old, so he wouldn't say anything for a few more weeks. Still, the feeling of Melanie's slight frame in his arms lingered in his mind. If only Shay had a body like hers.

A new thought dawned on him – Shay's birthday! He turned the page of the calendar and ticked off the coming weeks – five weeks away. "That's perfect!" His words came out loud in the silence of the empty office. Bringing up Google on his computer, Brett found the phone number for a nearby gym and within moments Shay's birthday gift was taken care of.

She'd be so thrilled that he remembered!

He would be equally thrilled to have his wife get back in shape.

***

Shay had been silent at dinner. Brett wondered what her problem was but chose not to ask. Finally, she broke the silence. "I don't think I'm quite ready to go back to church yet."

Brett dropped his fork and stared at her. "Forget it Shay. The Bible says to 'not forsake the assembling of ourselves together'. I have no interest in raising a bunch of heathens in this home. As an elder, it's expected that we be there every time the doors are open. The baby is over a week already – you don't need to be such a wimp.

The tears in Shay's eyes annoyed him. She was such a loser. Brett tried to swallow the frustrations down and left the table to get ready for church.

The elders meeting lasted less than fifteen minutes, but by the time it was over, Brett had volunteered to mow the church yard for the summer, lead a crew to empty the gutters and even promised to consider teaching a Young Marrieds Sunday School class. "So many admire you and Shay, Brett." Pastor Mike had said, "You're marriage is such a light to our congregation…and our community!"

Brett let the words soak in like a soft gentle rain. What an honor to be recognized for his efforts. Sure, he knew that he and Shay weren't perfect. Lord knows he'd been doing his best to get her to submit. The music pastor asked the congregation to open their hymn books as he lead them in worship.

Tis so sweet to trust in Jesus

Just to take Him at His word

The words faded out of Brett's mind as he returned to his troubled thoughts. Shay seemed so angry all the time and her attitude was not conducive to that of an elder's wife! What was he to do with her?

His contemplations were interrupted as his wife waddled up the aisle and sidestepped her way between the benches. Her turtleneck sweater hid the bruises on her arms, and she'd done a pretty good job with her makeup as well – he'd give her that.

Still, Brett shook his head... she looked awful. So unkempt. So fat! Didn't she care at all for his reputation? Brett looked down at his own neatly pressed suit and tie. He looked immaculate next to her frumpy appearance.

Holding the baby close to her, Shay settled in the seat beside her. A burst of disgust took over and Brett let his heel dig into the top of her foot. She swung and looked at him, but he kept his eyes pointed heavenward as he joined his baritone in at the chorus.

Jesus, Jesus how I trust Him

How I'd prove Him ore and ore

Jesus, Jesus, precious Jesus

Oh for grace, to trust Him more.

***

I'd like to think Brett and Shay's relationship is in the minority – and I hope I'm right. In all honesty, I debated heavily about including his story. But the truth is, just as the Orphan Spirit leads many people to do many sad and hurtful things, control is one of them. Brett's Spirit of Control manifests itself through abuse.

Throughout this book, we've talked about the Orphan Spirit's need to be in charge of situations. For Brett, he has no love or compassion for his wife or children – he is too busy feeding his hunger for perfection.

His call to leadership in the church placates his desire for affirmation but only to a certain degree. Along with the elevated status comes a new fear – the fear of being imperfect.

Caring more about his place in the congregation, Brett now uses his powers at home to dominate his wife and children. He incorrectly uses Scriptures as an excuse to beat his family into submission. When quoting the Bible doesn't work, he uses his strength.

The Spirit of Control is willing to bully those under them in order to maintain the status they think they deserve. They are excellent liars and able to manipulate situations to their favor. Notice that Brett had all but forgotten the abuse from the night before. The Orphan Spirit is unable to empathize with others and feels little remorse when causing another pain.

To them, people are little more than a step on the ladder of success.

While Brett was quick to volunteer for numerous jobs around the church, the Spirit of Control will only do the jobs he wants. Brett chose only jobs that, in his opinion, got him noticed or put him charge of people.

Obviously we need our churches maintained, classes taught and groups led – to do any of these jobs does not make one an Orphan Spirit! Please hear me in this!

It is not always the actions one does that reveal his current status in the Kingdom – orphan or son – no, it is his attitude and thought process behind those actions that make that determination.

The Spirit of Control rears its ugly head among Believers in a myriad of ways – not just through abuse. In fact, we catch a glimpse of it in many, if not all, of these stories. It is the primary cause of many failed relationships and church splits.

The need for control can also be the driving force behind the rules and regulations of any given denomination. Humanity can often find a way to control another's actions, but one can never control the state of the heart behind another's actions – therefore, rules do little to change hearts. It only breeds guilt, shame, separation and punishment.

Abba God longs to see His children walk in genuine love for one another, with a trust in Him that supersedes a personal need to control our brothers and sisters in the Kingdom.

Having lived a life of complete chaos and uncertainty, the orphan grasps at anything he or she can in order to maintain some semblance of certainty. The need for security and assurance is so great and once attained, the fear of losing it will drive the orphan to do crazy things.

Abba Daddy is our only source of security. The world we live in seems out of control at times... uncertain, scary and chaotic... and it's easy to cling to that which gives us so sense of peace and a confidence that all is well, but the body of Believers must be cautious to not put our trust in that which we can control, for in all reality, the only thing that is certain is God Himself. In a changing world, He never changes. He is rock solid, always present, ready to move on our behalf.

Furthermore, because we are united with Christ,
we have received an inheritance from God,
for He chose us in advance,
and He makes everything work out according to His plan.
Ephesians 1:11 NLT

CHAPTER 7
SPIRIT OF FATHERLESSNESS

Destiny was bored.

Restless.

The feeling was not unfamiliar to her, and she hated it.

She dug through her purse, looking for the remaining candy she had set aside earlier. No luck.

Tossing the bag aside, she climbed off her bed and continued shuffling through the mounds of laundry she'd piled on the chair earlier. Still nothing.

Forget the candy.

Annoyed now, Destiny made the short trip from her bedroom to the kitchen of her apartment and rummaged through the pantry hoping Abby had gone grocery shopping.

Score! She had! Destiny grabbed a snack cake, hesitated for a moment, and then grabbed another. Making a mental note to repay Abby, she plopped down on the sofa in the living room to eat and contemplate her boredom.

Ugh! She hated this! Hated the loneliness. Hated the monotony that was her life. Looking down at the empty wrappers on her plump belly, she sighed. And she hated her lack of self-control.

She'd expected the freshman fifteen to hit last year when she went to college but she hadn't expected the sophomore sixty!

"What else do you expect, Destiny?" Her voice broke the silence of the empty apartment as she brushed the remaining crumbs off her well-endowed chest. Tears pooled in the corner of her eyes and a lump collided with the remaining dessert in her throat.

"I HATE MY LIFE! I HATE IT, HATE IT, HATE IT, HATE IT!!" Pressing her beautifully manicured nails to her eyes, she tried to push back the tears. Breathing in deeply, she held the air in her chest and counted to ten before letting it out slowly.

"You gotta get ahold of yourself, girl!"

The boost of oxygen and self-reprimand joined forces with the sugar rush and Destiny felt better. Pushing herself up out of her chair, she had an idea.

Shoes! Yes! She'd head down to the mall and see what bargains she could find.

Gathering up the wrappers from her Twinkies, she shoved them down in the trash. Abby was going to be ticked – she just knew it. Her roommate hated when Destiny ate "her snacks." Thinking fast, Destiny grabbed the box of remaining Twinkies and hid them in her room. She'd just pick up a box to replace this one since she was going out anyway. If she hurried, she'd be done and back before Abby discovered what she'd done – crisis averted!

Destiny rushed to the bathroom, brushed her teeth and freshened up her makeup. Grabbing her new Gucci bag, she headed for the door. Just as her hands rested on the doorknob, she froze.

Wait-a-minute! A smile crawled slowly across her face.

She'd almost forgotten. Hadn't she seen a credit card envelope in the mail yesterday? She was sure she had. At the time, she'd tossed it into the trash telling herself one more credit card was *not* what she needed, but... the thought of additional funds began toying with her mind, easing the ache she felt inside.

Should she? She already had nine other cards – each near, or at, their limit. Destiny didn't need a masters degree to know how quickly nine credit cards with an average $2,000 credit limit was doing to her debt load.

The thought overwhelmed her. What should she do? She couldn't ask Mom for more money. She'd want to know why her waitressing job wasn't paying the bills and Destiny had no desire to try to explain the shopping addiction she'd acquired since leaving home.

Of course, she could always call Dad too, right? Anger boiled up in her gut at the thought of her father. The only thing he'd been present for in her life was her conception and the occasional $200 check around her birthday. It was guilt money and she knew it. The thought of accepting another dime from him turned her stomach.

No... no, she certainly wasn't desperate enough to ask that man for one red cent.

Destiny closed her eyes as the financial worries filled her mind, taking its place in her heart next to the restlessness, loneliness and fear.

FORGET IT! She was already so far gone financially, what would another $500 on top of her mountain of debt matter? Destiny found the envelope in the trash and ripped it open. $1,500 limit! Nice! She smiled, *ok, so what would another $1,000 matter?* She'd save the last $500 as an emergency fund.

The plan brought peace to her heart and a rush in her spirit. "Thank you, Jesus!" she sang to the empty room. Grabbing her bag once more, she turned and walked out the door.

***

When growing up in an orphanage, children have many caregivers. They are unfamiliar with the structure of having one mommy and one daddy to look to for guidance, comfort and security.

When a child is adopted, there is a struggle to adjust their thinking to having one mom and one dad. We watched this first hand when our friends brought their daughter, Eva, home from Uganda.

I was sitting by the pool with Carissa one afternoon watching our kids splash and play in the water. Carissa left her chair for a moment, for what reason, I can't recall. (Ask any mom of six and she'll tell you an afternoon by the pool does not include uninterrupted hours of just sitting!) While she was gone, Eva came toddling up to me. I was honored! She had only been home for a month or so and I hadn't expected her to come talk to a stranger.

Eva was cold and wet and, though her English was broken, I could make out the words, "I want a towel, mama."

My heart warmed. I loved that she felt so comfortable coming to me… and the fact that she called me 'Mama' was too cute.

Carissa didn't think so. When she saw what was happening, she quickly intervened. "Lynette, I know you mean well, and I'm not trying to offend you, but please send her to me when she needs help."

I was taken aback. I couldn't help but feel slightly offended and I didn't understand why my care and attention on her newly adopted child was unwanted.

Carissa went on, "Eva is so used to having many caregivers from her life in the orphanage. To her, anyone over five feet tall is someone that will offer care and security."

I nodded, the concept was new to me, but I was beginning to understand. Carissa went on, "Jon and I are doing all we can to get Eva to see us as her parents. She *needs* to recognize that *we* are the ones to come to for her needs…otherwise, she'll have so many more struggles later in life if she doesn't learn now to see us as her parents."

I understood now. I had never considered that this was something an orphan might face, and I couldn't help but began to see a correlation with the Orphan Spirit we find in our churches.

Destiny held a void in her heart... a void that began when she made a choice that would change her forever the summer she turned eighteen. Back before college... the weight gain... the debt...back before everything. There was that day. That one day that changed her forever.

She'd stared at the pregnancy test in disbelief. This was not how life was supposed to go! She had plans...dreams of journalism – hopefully travelling all over the world. She couldn't do that with a baby in tow.

Without telling a soul, Destiny had the tissue removed, not expecting any difficulties – but she awoke from the procedure different. Something wasn't right. She felt it in her soul... and she knew. Right then and there, she knew.

Call it a fetus. Call it tissue. Call it a blob all you want – but she knew! She knew she had just done the unthinkable – she had willingly allowed the murder of her child.

Oh, she tried to get over it – tried to tell herself it was for the best, but the shame became a part of who she is today – a shame that now manifests itself through loneliness, depression, and low self-esteem. Each time the discomfort rises to the surface of her soul, she runs to find comfort. Searching for a caregiver.

Destiny could be free from her turmoil if she chose to run to her Abba Daddy, but her shame tells her she can't. "He would be angry. He won't love you. He doesn't care."

Having never experienced a healthy relationship with her own dad, Destiny struggles to see God as a loving Father. To her, He is one who is distant, uncaring and unlikely to give her the desires of her heart. She remains on the outskirts of the Kingdom, longing for identity, belonging and love. Feeling Fatherless, Destiny desperately longs to find someone or something to offer her the care and comfort she so greatly desires.

There are many orphans fighting this same battle in the Kingdom. Orphan Spirits who don't know who their daddy is. Having become accustomed to looking to people and things as caregivers, they are easily pulled in by anything or anyone that will offer contentment in the moment.

Some find it in food, shopping or even in the arms of another. Always seeking for Mr. (or Mrs.) Right, they pour everything into one relationship after another. They fail to understand why things don't work out... and are left condemning themselves when the shame of multiple lovers consumes them.

For others, it's alcohol or drugs.

For some, it's ministry. That's right! Ministry.

Consumed by the empty place in their heart, the Orphan Spirit can find fulfillment in pouring themselves into ministering within the walls of the church. While it appears holy and good, it is done for selfish gain - the approval of others. This is one of the hardest to identify because the actions are acceptable. Even so, the motivation is the same as her orphan spirited siblings who are running from one relationship to another or addicted to drugs. For this orphan spirit, they have simply discovered a more acceptable drug of choice.

The daughter of Christ knows where ultimate peace and love is found. Does she buy food, and shoes and Gucci bags? Sure. Does she serve in the church? Absolutely! But it isn't done to replace a void deep inside. Instead, she rests in the presence of her Abba Daddy - knowing He alone can fill the empty places of her heart.

She sees Him as the ultimate Father, provider and source of comfort. He is enough!

Knowing she is His daughter, she is able to live free and unhindered by an inner hunger for love and affection.

I will not leave you fatherless.
John 14:18 GNV

CHAPTER 8
SPIRIT OF INSECURITY

"Hey, how's it going?"

Kathy checked her spelling, added a smiling emoticon and let her finger hover over the send button. She hesitated for a moment, then just for good measure, added two more smiley faces and punched 'send'.

Several seconds ticked by until the phone messenger showed that the message had been read.

Kathy waited.

Soon, a minute had passed and still no response from Alisa. Why wasn't she answering? Maybe she was driving.

Kathy flicked open her Facebook app and began scrolling through the newsfeed. Someone had posted pictures of their new baby. Aww.. what a cutie. Next, an article about a pizza place refusing service to gays… Hmm.. Kathy kept scrolling when suddenly there was Alisa's face, right there on the screen.

Alisa *and* their mutual friend, Sara!

Kathy looked closer to read the caption. "Coffee and girl time! #justwhatineed"

Really? Were they serious right now?

The post had been made fifteen minutes earlier – which explained why Alisa hadn't answered Kathy's text.

Disgusted, Kathy clicked off the screen, tossed her phone onto the couch and stomped out to the kitchen. Yanking the dishwasher door open, she began shoving the clean dishes into the cabinets – slamming the doors closed as she worked.

What was their problem anyway? Why hadn't they invited her? *I thought we were friends!*

An idea entered Kathy's mind and without a moment's hesitation, she left the half-emptied dishwasher and went back for her phone. Finding the post on Facebook again, she opened the comment box, "Looks like fun. Love me some girl time! <3"

She stared at the comment, and then backspaced until the heart was removed. She wanted to sound nice – just not too nice. Pressing send, Kathy felt satisfied. Now at least they'd know she'd seen what they were doing…without her.

She was just shoving the phone in her pocket when a text came in.

Alisa!

"Hey you! It's going good! How have you been?" A simple smiley face was added to the end of the message and Kathy wondered if that meant she was really happy or just pretending to be happy.

"I'm good. Saw you went for coffee today. Looked like fun". Normally she would have used an exclamation point but not with the way she was feeling right now. It sounded silly, but Alisa didn't deserve even the effort of an exclamation point or happy emoticons. Not when she had chosen another friend over her!

Ding ding.

Another message appeared on the screen. "Yeah! We had a great time. Sara is so sweet! She's been wanting to take me out for my birthday and it finally worked today."

"Your birthday? Umm... does she know that was two months ago?"

"Of course, silly. We've both been busy, that's all. So what's up? Had you wanted something earlier?"

Kathy stared at the message. What was that supposed to mean? Was she upset? The idea was both empowering and alarming to Kathy. In some ways, she wanted Alisa to feel the misery she now felt, but at the same time, the fear of losing her friendship with Alisa terrified her.

"Yeah, just thought it would be fun to go bowling tonight. You in?" Kathy hadn't thought of bowling until just now, but it was a good plan and if Alisa had time for Sara, she must not have anything going on today.

Once again, Kathy could see that Alisa had read the message and wondered why there was no response. Irritated, she pushed the phone into her pocket and went to the bathroom.

As she stood at the sink washing her hands, she let her gaze sweep over her hair, makeup and body. She liked what she saw. She looked good. Real good.

Pulling her phone back out of her pocket, she searched for the perfect angle to reflect the beauty she saw. A tug on her shirt here provided just a hint of cleavage, a brush of her hair there, suck in that gut and… perfect.

Kathy studied the photo and hit delete. Try again. Eleven pictures later, she finally settled on one she liked. Back to the living room, she sank into the recliner and began playing around with her editing app in an effort to enhance the beauty of the photo even more.

Her eyes sparkled back at her from the photo. *Cute, I like it!* With a smile on her face, Kathy tapped out her caption "Shine for Jesus" and uploaded it to her Facebook wall.

Switching over to her text messages, she found Alisa's name. "Hello?"

No answer.

Five minutes later, Kathy was starting to sweat. What was up? Should she ask Alisa if she was mad? Did Alisa not want to be her friend? Was she still with Sara? Maybe they were going out tonight and, even now, trying to figure out the perfect excuse to ditch Kathy.

Kathy's irritation with her friend was alleviated by the three likes she'd received on her selfie already.

Kathy stayed snuggled up in her chair watching the compliments and likes roll in. There weren't as many as she'd hoped. And they didn't take away the pain of rejection she felt from Alisa.

But at least it helped.

***

It's a common theme, perhaps – the need for affirmation. The need for value and love.

With the advent of social media, the Orphan Spirit has discovered a new tool to aid in his quest for identity. It doesn't happen only on social media – no, the Orphan Spirit has been around much longer than Facebook and Instagram but you don't have to search long to find the faces of spiritual orphans begging for a bite of the bread of admiration and applause.

Within the Orphan Spirit is a susceptibility to rejection. Their spirit tells them they're not good enough. Never good enough. They carry with them a fear of being abandoned, rejected and exposed.

Could people still love them if they knew, really knew, all their inmost thoughts?

While their brothers and sisters extend love and friendship, the relationships often become strained. The orphan's constant need for approval and acknowledgment claws at their siblings, draining the life out of the friendship.

When boundaries are erected, the orphan feels sorry for themselves and the cycle of 'I'm not good enough, you don't love me, tell me I have worth, you let me down, I'm not good enough' continues.

The insecure orphan must stop depending on frail humanity for self-worth. Mankind is weak and imperfect... and no matter how sincere we are we fail one another. How many friendships, marriages and other relationships could be saved if each individual were to find their value through the eyes of their Father. Instead, we look to one another to affirm that we are thought of, adored, loved, and valuable – and while we should do those things for one another – we cannot do them perfectly.

When others fail to meet the expectations of the Spirit of Insecurity, the orphan convinces herself that the problem lies with the other person, rather than with her. Once she's found another individual to agree with her, the slander begins. Soon, all that is left are the bloody wounds of a broken relationship...and no one the happier for it.

Sons and daughters know that their identity, adoration and self-worth are best found when looking to their Father. He is the only One who is capable of complete and perfect love.

Kingdom kids enjoy social media, emoticons, friendships, coffee breaks, and yes, even the occasional selfie. But they are not dependent on these things for their source of joy. Instead, they can live free of care, knowing they have a place in the Kingdom and it matters not what others think.

But you are a chosen race,
a royal priesthood,
a holy nation,

a people for His own possession,
that you may proclaim
the excellencies of Him who called you out of darkness
into His marvelous light.
1 Peter 2:9 ESV

CHAPTER 9
SPIRIT OF FALSE HUMILITY

Teresa looked over her list of things to do.

Stop by the bank

Pick up gift for the Benson's baby

Deliver meal to the Bensons

Visit Sister Pam

Stop by the church to make copies for Sunday School

Take Kenzie to dentist appointment

She sighed.

Was there ever a break? A glance at the calendar reminded Teresa that Worship practice was tonight. Grabbing a pen, she added one more item to her already overwhelming list.

Make song list

That part wouldn't be so hard. If there was one thing Teresa loved doing, it was leading worship. Plus, she had just found a new song that complimented her voice range and she couldn't wait to sing it for the church on Sunday.

Looking over her list once more, she made a quick decision. Maybe she'd mail a card to Sister Pam instead of stopping by. A new thought struck her and she hesitated. On the other hand...

Leaving the list as is, she called for Kenzie and the two rushed out the door.

Kenzie slouched in the passenger seat of the car, her headphones firmly in place and her phone to her nose.

Typical.

Teresa wheeled the car through the bank drive thru in record time before circling the parking lot of their local Target. Back in the car, she gently folded the baby blanket and tucked it into a gift bag, along with some pampers.

They still had some time before the dentist appointment. *Perfect!* Teresa smiled. *Just enough time to stop by the nursing home and visit Sister Pam.*

Kenzie whined when she saw where they were going, "Nooooooo...! Do I have to go in there?"

"Yes ma'am, you do! And you're going to be happy about it too!"

"Whatever!"

Teresa bit her tongue, deciding to ignore the disrespect from her thirteen year old. Glancing at the sky, she shot a silent prayer, hoping He was listening. "Lord, help me not kill this child!"

She knew she wouldn't but some days she wondered if *she'd* survive the teen years.

"Why do we gotta visit her anyway?" Apparently, Kenzie wasn't done complaining yet. "She doesn't even know who we are… and besides, it stinks in there!"

"Then plug your nose." Teresa knew she wasn't winning Parent of the Year awards with her technique but she was tired and, frankly, didn't care. The whining got to her though. Who cares if Kenzie didn't go inside. She'd leave her to enjoy her music in the car – leaving Teresa to enjoy a few moments of peace and quiet. "Fine. Stay out here then. Just keep the doors locked. I'll try to make it quick."

That got a smile from her daughter and Teresa walked briskly into Fair Haven Manor alone. The hallways were quiet, with only a few elderly folks nodding off in their wheelchairs. Teresa entered Sister Pam's room quietly and saw the woman was also dozing in her bed.

Alzheimer's had been taking its toll on Pam's frail body, and Teresa knew their conversation would be limited at best. Touching her arm, Teresa tried to rouse Pam from her sleep.

Sister Pam opened her eyes and stared blankly at Teresa. "Who are you?"

"It's me, Sister Pam. Teresa Shaffer. Rick and Bonnie's daughter.

Silence.

Teresa smiled down at the woman who'd been a pillar in the church for so many years. "How are you?" Teresa's words were loud in the quiet room.

"I still can't find that roasting pan." Sister Pam stared at the cabinet along the north wall for a moment before closing her eyes once again.

Teresa noticed the clock on the wall. It seemed silly to leave already, but Sister Pam seemed pretty checked out and was unlikely to notice anyway.

"Well, I just wanted to stop by and say hi. I hope you're doing well."

Sister Pam opened her eyes as though seeing her for the first time, "Who are you?"

Teresa sighed.

A nurse was walking by in the hall and Teresa flagged her down, "Would you mind taking a picture of Sister Pam and I before I leave?"

"Sure, not a problem," the nurse stepped into the room and took Teresa's phone.

Teresa bent near Sister Pam's face, smiled, and was soon rushing towards the exit to her car. Uploading her picture to Facebook, she tapped out a quick "So blessed to visit sweet Sister Pam this morning". Tagging herself at Fair Haven Manor, she hit 'Post', and climbed into the car.

The dentist visit was over within an hour and Teresa returned Kenzie home where she pulled together the meal for the Bensons and raced back out the door. Checking her phone, she noticed numerous notifications on her Facebook app. Taking a moment to open them, she smiled in satisfaction at the amount of comments that filled the page. Most mentioned how much they loved and appreciated Sister Pam but Teresa's favorites were Sister Mary, Pastor John's wife, and Sister Annalise, their deacon's wife.

Both women complimented Teresa on her thoughtfulness to stop by and visit the elderly woman.

Good! That visit was worth my time after all. Teresa drove the three miles to the Benson's home and made short work of dropping off the meal for the young family. She made sure to gush over the baby an appropriate length of time. Another quick photo of her holding the baby was uploaded to Facebook and she was out the door.

By the time she had arrived at the church, Heather Benson had already liked her picture and thanked her for bringing them a meal.

Another spark of joy shot through Teresa's heart. How she loved serving!

Gathering her folder of Sunday School papers, Teresa nearly skipped across the church parking lot. She rushed past a janitor in the foyer, nodded at a group of women near the drinking fountain and continued down the hall to the secretary's office.

"Hi, Teresa!" Teresa stopped short, nearly bumping into Michelle Walker who was just coming out of the Pastor's office. Behind her was Sister Mary, both holding folders of their own and pleasant smiles on their faces.

"Looks like you've had quite a busy day," Sister Mary said as she gave Teresa a quick hug.

"Yeah, it's been crazy." She smiled. "Crazy, but good."

"Well, we sure appreciate you." Sister Mary smiled. "You are such a blessing to so many!"

"Thank you, I'm happy to help." Sister Mary's kind words bubbled up in Teresa, making the stress from her busy day melt away into nothing.

Sister Mary turned back to Heather, "Oh, and one more thing, Heather. We'll need to remember to ask the Hospitality Committee to provide decorations for the tables as well."

"You're right! Great point!" Heather grabbed her phone and began tapping away, likely making a note to herself. Teresa looked confused, not knowing what the conversation was about.

Sister Mary noticed her confusion, "Oh Teresa, great news! Heather has offered to head up our Women's Conference this year! Isn't that wonderful?"

Confusion turned to dismay, which in turn became disgust.

Heather? Heather Jacobs! In *charge* of the Pleasant Valley Bible Women's Conference? Seriously?

Teresa plastered the biggest fake smile she could muster onto her face and hoped her voice matched their excitement. "Really? Wow. Yeah, that is wonderful!"

She listened as they chattered on about their plans. The speaker – some author from Illinois (*not really a big ticket name*), the theme – Renewing of the Mind (*sounds dumb*) and the hopes that many would come and be blessed (*yeah, yeah.*)

"When is it again?" Teresa asked, already certain she would be unable to attend.

"May 3rd and 4th. We love that it's right before Mother's Day!"

The gushing, oohing and aahing was almost more than Teresa could take. Counterfeit joy remained firmly on her face as she pulled up her calendar and flipped to May. The white squares were blank, but Sister Mary and Heather couldn't see that.

"Ohhhh, bummer!" Teresa smile faded away as she wrinkled up her nose. "We already promised Terry's mom that we'd come down to visit that weekend. We knew we couldn't go over Mother's Day weekend, so we hoped to go that weekend instead."

Disappointment filled Sister Mary's eyes, "Oh that is a bummer. Well, don't you stress about it. We would love to have you here, but we know how important it is to spend time with our elderly ones. But who am I to tell you that? You do so good in that area!"

The kind words were welcome but did little to restore the joy to Teresa's heart. She knew they hadn't promised her in-laws a weekend visit... but they would now. The last thing she wanted to do was hang around the church that weekend listening to everyone fussing to high heaven over Heather's amazing women's conference. The thought nearly made her ill.

No. Teresa Shaffer would certainly not be present at the Pleasant Valley Bible Women's Conference this year.

The ladies could "renew their minds" just fine without her.

***

Of all the ways an Orphan Spirit permeates our churches, this is the least evident, but, perhaps, the most nauseating to the world around us – it is The Spirit of False Humility.

Who doesn't want a church full of willing workers?

Teresa is available, ready and willing to serve, but her motivation stinks! She is one who appears holy, yet her main focus is to gain approval from those around her – especially those in leadership.

To secure their place in the family, an orphan can be found working feverishly, needing to stand out. The memories of being a nobody are fresh in the Orphan Spirit's minds and they will do all they can to make a name for themselves.

Spiritual Orphans can be much like the older son we see in the story of the Prodigal Son. He is determined to perform well and overcompensates by working hard. He measures his position with the Father based on the failures of his brother.

He knows he should grieve when his brother or sisters disappoint, yet inside, he cannot help but celebrate their weaknesses. When one sibling is lifted up to a place of promotion, the Orphan Spirit feels the sting of rejection and struggles to support and promote their brother or sister.

Why is it so damaging to the church?

Because it takes the focus off Christ… and places it on ourselves. At the same time, it breaks down family bonds and stirs up dissension.

An orphan often has little choice but to watch out for number one. Giving up any of their meager possessions is a huge loss. When God the Father chose to adopt us as His own, He invites us to come into His rest and experience the fullness of His undeserved grace and favor. In His Kingdom, He provides all that we need and all that we do should be prompted by a desire to bring *HIM* glory – not ourselves. He calls us to lay aside our box of false humility and pride and trust Him for our value.

The Orphan Spirit never feels as though they truly belong. Though given love, possessions, home… even a new name - it's never enough. She needs constant reassurance that she is wanted. She will serve zealously in her attempt to gain the admiration of others and, she hopes, God Almighty.

The daughter of Christ serves out of love and compassion, at peace knowing that God loves her in spite of her works. She recognizes that there is nothing she can do, no task she can accomplish that will cause God to love her more – or less.

He simply loves her.

Just as she is.

And it's that knowledge that compels her to serve her Abba Father. She feels a security in knowing that His love doesn't go away based on her performance.

She knows He doesn't *need* her to be His child.

He just *wants* her to be His child.

Not because of who she is... or what she's done, but because in His great love, He sees her and loves her as His own. She was reason enough to bankrupt heaven – even *before* she was capable of leading worship, teaching Sunday School, delivering baby meals and visiting the elderly.

Does He still want His children to do those things? Yes!

But stop doing it for you.

Do it for Him.

At one time all of us lived to please our old selves. We gave in to what our bodies and minds wanted. We were sinful from birth like all other people and would suffer from the anger of God. But God had so much loving-kindness. He loved us with such a great love. Even when we were dead because of our sins, He made us alive by what Christ did for us. You have been saved from the punishment of sin by His loving-favor. God raised us up from death when He raised up Christ Jesus. He has given us a place with Christ in the heavens. He did this to show us through all the time to come the great riches of His loving-favor. He has shown us His kindness through Christ Jesus.
Ephesians 2:3-7 NLV

CHAPTER 10
SPIRIT OF DECEPTION

Jared rushed through the hallway of the church corridor. He glanced at his watch while pushing out a deep breath. Of all times, why did he have to be late tonight?

He turned right at the corner and then right again as he entered one of the newly constructed classrooms. Eight other members of the congregation already surrounded the table in the center of the room. They all looked up as he slid into a seat, but no one said a word as they continued listening to the church secretary read over the minutes from last month's board meeting.

"After fire alarm final inspection, there is still need for a full final inspection to attain the building permit. Upon approval, full payment must be rendered to the builder." Sherry's voice droned on, something about a sprinkler system, donating old cabinets to Habitat for Humanity or the like. Yada, yada, yada…

Jared hated this part of the meeting. What was the point of reading the minutes out loud anyway? Everyone had a copy of it in their hands, right? And last he checked, everyone in the room knew how to read.

He stifled another sigh and skimmed down through to the agenda.

Cal – update on building permit

Roberta – report on 45ᵗʰ anniversary celebration

Jared – options for pulpit and altar table

Jared felt the blood drain out of his face and his heart skipped a beat. A word ran through his mind and he quickly glanced around the room, hoping to God he hadn't said it out loud. His fellow board members were still listening to Sherry reading the final paragraph of the minutes and no one seemed to notice his discomfort.

What should he do? He'd completely forgotten that he'd offered… no, insisted that he be the one to choose a custom builder for the new pulpit and altar table they'd hoped to purchase before the congregation's highly anticipated 45ᵗʰ anniversary celebration.

Crud! Double crud!

Jared pulled up the calendar on his phone and realized that the anniversary celebration was only three weeks away.

What was wrong with him? He'd been given this assignment six months ago already and had insisted it would be no trouble at all.

Nothing was wrong with him! Jared shook his head as though to remove the disturbing thought. Cal glanced at him curiously and Jared flashed him his winning smile, hoping to assure him that all was well. Nothing was wrong at all. He just wasn't one who needed half a year to complete a project. He still had plenty of time.

Moving his eyes back up the page, Jared knew he had about thirty minutes until they'd be looking his way. He grabbed his phone and pulled up Google. A quick search gave him hundreds, if not thousands of pulpits to choose from. He picked out his favorite three, saved their images then flipped over to his email app.

Roberta was talking now and Jared was careful to look up on occasion and nod, all the while hoping it looked like he was taking notes on the meeting.

Once the images were centered on his email page, he flipped back and quickly copied and pasted the price for each one.

It was looking better all the time. Back to his photo gallery, Jared found the church logo and added it to the top of his email.

Done!

It wasn't the best way to make up a presentation – even for a smart phone, but in his panic, the email seemed like the easiest option.

In the address box he typed out C H U and immediately the church printer email address appeared. Punching send, Jared sighed in relief when he heard the copier kick in across the hallway.

Cal hadn't been talking more than a minute when Jared politely excused himself to the restroom. Ducking into the church office, he grabbed his email off the printer, trimmed off the email address and made nine copies, taking care to make it look as professional as possible.

He chuckled as he looked over the paper. Not bad. Not bad at all.

Returning to the meeting, Jared was soon presenting his pulpit options to the board. Cal seemed unimpressed and his lack of approval goaded Jared. Choosing to ignore him, Jared pulled phrases out of the air, thankful for his ability to ad lib, as he won over the hearts of everyone on the board.

Everyone, it seemed, except Cal.

"I'm confused, Jared." Cal began, "I don't mean to doubt you, but this has little to no information at all." Cal paused for a moment as though uncertain how to speak his mind. "For example, are these all from the same company?"

"No. No, of course not," Jared chuckled, his tone held just enough condescension to make his point while (hopefully) turning gaining some support from the others. "If only it was that easy, right?" Jared threw a wink at Roberta. The elderly woman nodded her agreement with a chuckle of her own.

"No, my research took me to three separate companies but rather than choosing the pulpit myself, I decided to wait and get everyone's vote."

"So what companies are these from?"

Really? He was gonna go there?

Jared hesitated for only a moment, "I won't bore you with all that info tonight. I know we all have families at home that we want to get to, so I just brought the bare necessities – the looks and the price."

Again, Cal spoke up, "My concern though, Jared, is our time frame. Are you saying you still haven't ordered these? And I thought we were going to go with a custom builder… someone local."

Jared thought fast. "Actually, yes, they are ordered. All three of them. I mean… they are all on hold until tomorrow. I just have to call and cancel the two we don't want. Like I said before, I wanted to allow all of you the privilege of helping choose the pulpit. And yes, a local builder was mentioned, but with concern over the budget, I wanted to present these alternative options to you as they are much more affordable."

"Ok… so how much would it be if we went through the a custom builder?"

Cal was relentless. His barrage of questions annoyed Jared and he knew he needed to wrap this up before it all fell apart. "There are several builders in the area, but the ones I spoke to are all behind schedule. From my understanding, they wouldn't be able to get the pulpit built in time."

"They told you that six months ago?" Cal's eyes told Jared he was on to him. Jared held his gaze, unwilling to back down.

"Yes. That's correct." Jared kept his voice steady, although he wanted to tell Cal what a jerk he was being…and maybe punch him in the throat. "Custom furniture is in high demand and I've been contacting various builders within a fifty mile radius, but, unfortunately, there is no one that is in our price range and or able to build it within our time frame." Jared knew his voice was dripping with sarcasm by the time he was finished speaking. And that this was the biggest lie he'd told so far tonight, but he didn't care. He'd meant to do it... he just hadn't had time. Besides, he told himself, what matters most is a person's intentions, right? Cal had issues! He needed to learn a little more about giving grace to people in Jared's opinion.

The ladies were nodding understandingly towards Jared but Cal was unmoved. "So what about the altar table? I don't see any information here on your... um...presentation."

Jared's blood ran cold. He'd had all he could take. Working to maintain his composure, he went on to assure the board members that a coordinating altar table was available for each pulpit listed. Once chosen, he would simply tack on a table and all would be well.

Checking his watch, Jared brought his time to a sudden close, "I hope you all don't mind me slipping out a little early. I've been wanting to stop by the hospital to pray with Hank and Joyce... was hoping I'd have time tonight yet."

Heads began nodding. "Yes, yes, of course. Please go... and send them our love. Tell them we're praying for them."

As soon as the evening air hit his face, Jared drew in a deep breath. He'd survived! Now for a quick stop at the hospital, and he could maybe get home in time for some Monday Night Football.

It wasn't until he entered the hospital parking lot that he realized the board had never decided on a pulpit. As soon as he'd mentioned Hank, everyone seemed to have forgotten all talk about 45th celebrations, pulpits and altar tables as the sobering reminder that a forty-something father of five was about to meet his maker.

He supposed he shouldn't be relieved that it was the tragic situation of Hank lying in a hospital bed succumbing to cancer that had benefited him that night. But it couldn't be helped.

Hank would never know and no one had been hurt in the process.

Quite simply, it was what it was.

***

Jared represents the deceptive nature of an Orphan Spirit. In his desperation to retain his position and the admiration of his fellow board members, he willingly lied about the current status of the project for which he was responsible.

Jared thinks he's home-free when he leaves the meeting, but he will have some difficult days ahead as he struggles to maintain the web of lies he has created. He is unwilling to admit that he has failed – that thought alone drives him further away from the truth of the matter and he hates anyone who calls him out in his deceit.

The deceptive spirit depends on their ability to win people with their charm, wit and amicable personality, but stand in their way and you will find yourself at the wrong end of a fight.

Take Cal for example. He sensed something wasn't right and asked for more details. To protect himself, Jared did what the Orphan Spirit is prone to do – he went on the attack. He mocked Cal – subtly, but enough to get his point across and turn the hearts of his brothers and sisters away from Cal...and towards himself.

The deceptive nature found in the heart of the spiritual orphan causes more pain inside the Kingdom than a majority of the other attributes of the Orphan Spirit. It promotes distrust, anger, betrayal and hatred. It kindles division and devastates relationships, leaving in its wake untold destruction.

The Spirit of Deception cares only for his personal gain. He must survive. He must thrive. He must succeed. Should anyone stand in his way, they must be eliminated.

Jared sees Cal as a threat to his position in the Kingdom, therefore during the halftime commercials of the football game that night, Jared begins to conjure up what stories he can say and who he can say them to. Oh, they'll be truthful...for the most part. He might tweak it here and there... might leave some sentences hanging, allowing those listening to fill in the blanks with their own imagination.

Jared had a few things on Cal...and after the stunt he pulled tonight, Jared thinks it might be time to pull that information out of his sack of tricks. Information he'd tucked away some years ago...information he'd use to ruin Cal's pristine reputation - or at the very least, tarnish it.

That's how the Spirit of Deception works. Caring little for those around them, they use their friends, their colleagues, fellow staff members, their leaders, the elderly and children – even their own if need be, to reach their desired end result.

Sons and daughters live their lives with humility - willing to admit when they are wrong. Sons and daughters see their need for redemption. Let's look for an example at two men in the Bible who knew Jesus on a personal level.

Peter and Judas had several things in common. First, they were both disciples of Jesus. They both had lived life with Him for three years. Both appeared completely devoted to Him. And both betrayed Jesus at the time of His death.

Ugh… *betrayal.*

Cut-to-the-heart *betrayal!*

Yet this is where their stories take on a sharp contrast from one another. Judas hangs himself while Peter finds forgiveness.

It's a curious thing - both had lied. Both had done things that would benefit themselves while causing great pain to Jesus. So why did one die while the other went on to live a dynamic life for God? Why the difference?

To find the answer, we must look back earlier in the story. Back to when Judas took the bread at the Last Supper. Jesus was offering a new covenant to His followers, yet the moment Judas takes the bread of covenant, he leaves the scene and isn't heard from again until that night when he leads the High Priests and Pharisees to find Jesus is in the Garden of Gethsemane. There, Judas kisses Jesus in his final act of betrayal, signaling to those with him that this Jesus of Nazareth.

The kiss and the bread signify that Judas wanted intimacy without covenant. He wanted the benefits of Kingdom living, without any sacrifice of his own. The sacrifice of giving up what he thought he needed. The sacrifice of making himself available to receive God's best for his life.

The problem for Judas is that humanity is created with an innate desire for restoration. Having been made in the image of God – a God of justice, we too long for justice. We long for redemption. Judas, overwhelmed with guilt, chose to create his own redemption – and he hung himself.

Peter was also overwhelmed by the weight of his sin. He had done exactly what Jesus had predicted, and had loudly denied Jesus three times as the Messiah stood accused. Luke 22:61 tells of the moment when Peter had denied Jesus for the third time. Immediately, there was the sound of a rooster crowing. Peter looked up, and at that moment, Jesus turned and the two shared a look that no one else there could have understood.

Oh, the devastation of deception. The sting of betrayal! Imagine the depth of pain that one look must have held – for both Peter and Jesus.

Now Peter was in the same condition as Judas – he had deceived those around him, ultimately betraying the One who loved him most. Now it was Peter who needed restoration. But rather than create his own redemption as Judas had done, Peter was filled with humility and remorse. The Bible tells us that he went out and wept bitterly.

Three days later, upon Jesus resurrection, we find Peter racing to find Jesus, desperate for complete restoration. Because he took on a spirit of humility and repentance, Peter experienced the benefits of being a son – he was forgiven, redeemed and restored. Jesus loved him no less for what he had done, and Peter went on to live a life of one who remembered where he had once been… and what being adopted into the Kingdom meant for him. He left the Orphan Spirit behind and experienced full redemption.

He had known the weight of sin…felt the sting of remorse…and received the gift of forgiveness. He now had something he needed to tell the world!

And that's exactly what he did.

The Book of Acts tells story after story of Peter's power-packed life after he found freedom from his past, and turned away from the spirit of deception. Peter's experience was an important reminder to him throughout his life of what redemption looks like, and it was that experience that gave him the ability to love those who had caused great pain to others.

How he must have grieved the day Ananias and Sapphira stood before him, filled with pride, trying to deceive the leaders of the church. He had been in their shoes and knew the temptation… the temptation to say just the right words to gain the outcome you so desire… and he knew what their deception would gain them.

Obviously a lie doesn't lead to certain death, but Peter understood that when we refuse to acknowledge our faults, it truly does lead to death…the death of relationships, the death of dreams, and the death of ministries.

Kingdom living calls us to humble ourselves and admit when we're wrong…and that…that will lead to life.

It only takes a spark, remember, to set off a forest fire. A careless or wrongly placed word out of your mouth can do that. By our speech we can ruin the world, turn harmony to chaos, throw mud on a reputation, send the whole world up in smoke and go up in smoke with it, smoke right from the pit of hell.
James 3:5-6 MES

CHAPTER 11
SPIRIT OF HOPELESSNESS

Staring out the window, Barbara sighed.

What was the point?

Nothing had changed. And nothing would change.

What did she have to look forward but misery piled on misery. Sorrow added to doom.

It was everywhere – in the news, in her family, at work, the gym, her Sunday School class and now this. Her home.

Barbara watched as her husband of thirty-seven years loaded the final box into the back of his crossover. Closing the back hatch, he turned and let his eyes meet hers.

There was nothing left to say.

It was over.

Completely over.

Thirty-seven years of what? Certainly not wedded bliss!

Eric opened his mouth as if to say something but then closed it again. Climbing into the driver's seat, he started the engine, closed the door... and drove away.

Unable to hold back the tears any longer, Barbara buried her head in her hands and wept.

***

Little changed in the long year following Eric's departure. Barbara made several attempts to pull herself together but found no reason to do so. Most days were spent grieving what once was. Those years when she, Eric and the boys had enjoyed summer nights in the backyard. They had tossed the football back and forth while she tended her garden.

Those days were gone forever.

They, Eric and the boys, were gone forever.

One by choice, two by death.

Perhaps that was when it all fell apart – that long ago day Bruce nervously sat his parents down and told them that he was sorry. He loved them, after all. Knew their religious beliefs, but...he couldn't help it.

He was gay.

The shouting that ensued was devastating.

The words thrown out in anger, cruel.

The tears, endless.

The relationship between father and son, fractured beyond repair.

Bruce left that night. Eric said he didn't care, "No child of mine is going to be gay!" He was after all, a minster of the Gospel! He had a reputation…a standard to uphold. He'd done his level best - how could God let this happen now when they had served Him so faithfully for so many years?

David took it especially hard –the broken relationship. He and Bruce had entered her world only fourteen minutes apart – identical down to the small mole on the back of their necks. The loss was difficult for him and with the unexpected exit of both his brother and best friend, David struggled to find his way.

Several months after Bruce left, David joined the Army and, just like that, Eric and Barbara were empty nesters. The big house and backyard full of memories was no longer needed, so they placed a For Sale sign in the yard and moved to a tiny home four blocks away.

The years passed – David succeeded in the military, eventually becoming a captain. His parents beamed with pride over his accomplishments. How Barbara wished Bruce would be standing next to her in the family photos. But he was never there. Never invited. Eric had put his foot down and she knew there was little wisdom in questioning his authority.

Then one day, the phone rang. To her complete surprise, it was Bruce. He'd found her phone number on the Internet, he'd said. And was it ok that he called? Yes, yes, she'd assured him. Was it really already four years since she'd last seen him? How she missed her boy!

They talked for an hour until Barbara had heard Eric's car pull in the drive. Hoping Bruce would understand, she begged him to call again, but she needed to go before Eric came through the door.

Bruce understood.

Eric hadn't noticed a difference in her voice, although she knew she sounded happier. She tried to keep her excitement at bay, knowing Eric wouldn't approve of her talking to their son.

She needn't have worried. Eric was in the middle of writing a sermon series for their tiny congregation. She glanced over his shoulder, not surprised to see he was coming at his favorite subject yet again – Death and Destruction, the title read. Beneath it were the words, Earth's Final Days.

Barbara picked up his empty coffee cup and moved towards the sink. She knew better than to suggest a different topic. Eric took his calling to warn sinners of the coming doom seriously . Trouble was, a scarce number of people found their way into the pews of their little church each Sunday, leaving Eric with only a faithful few to preach to.

Barbara remembered the sermons he used to preach – back when they were filled with hope and encouragement. But after Bruce's highly unexpected and very unwelcome announcement, Eric had changed.

Even his sermons had changed.

Maybe it was out a genuine love and concern for his son's salvation, but the fact was, Eric was using fear tactics in order to entice people to the throne of God. Barbara wasn't convinced it was working.

She would never admit it to Eric but she was tired of hearing it. Tired of hearing the endless predictions, tired of the warnings of the impending sorrow, tired of wondering what tomorrow might bring. "I'm going to the garden," she tossed into the quiet air but Eric never stirred.

Sighing, she opened the back door and stepped outside. Looking up into the darkness, she gazed at the gold specks littering the sky. It had been so good to talk to Bruce. She wished she could have talked longer. Wished she could share her excitement with Eric.

Barbara walked along the edge of her backyard flowergardens. They sat unattended, dwindling from lack of care. Her plan had been to fill them with perennials when they bought the home but as the truth of Eric's sermons hit home, she felt there was little reason to plant tulips, hydrangeas and columbine – after all, she'd likely not even be here to enjoy it. That was four years ago already. "Humph… how stupid." Her voice was soft, barely a whisper, "Imagine how nice they would be if I'd planted them when we moved here."

***

Several more years went by. Eric continued to preach doom and gloom, Bruce snuck calls in on occasion, David got sent to Iraq and Barbara prayed daily for his safety, Bruce's salvation…and the Rapture.

It was early February the day the news came. Barbara was home alone when she heard the knock at the door. They stood there, solemn, hats in hand. Barbara screamed in horror and tried to shut the door. Tried to shut out the world. Tried to shut out the words no mother ever wants to hear.

Collapsing under the weight of the crushing grief, Barbara cried out with a pain she had never known before. No! It couldn't be! It couldn't be! Not him! Not her David!

The uniformed men did their best to console her until Eric returned home. The rest of the night was spent in separate rooms, with only her muffled sobs breaking the silence.

Bruce came to the funeral. Eric ignored him. Barbara clung to him. He was thin. Too thin. Barbara begged him to stay but the tension was too great. He hugged her one last time as they stood among the gravestones and then, without a word to his father, Bruce turned and walked away.

Only a month had passed before Bruce called her. "Mom. I'm in town. We need to talk." Barbara's heart froze. She couldn't take anymore bad news, but try as she might, she couldn't shake the bad feeling in her gut. It was worse than any fear she'd felt before. Something was wrong. Terribly wrong.

Bruce was sitting near a window at the local coffee shop. When Barbara walked in, he smiled at her and motioned for her to follow him to a back corner booth. Barbara smiled at him, "How are you, son? I've missed you!" Bruce's smile was thin. Forced. He sat there for a moment as though deciding what to say.

"This isn't easy for me to tell you, mom."

"What? What is it, Bruce?" Her voice held desperate fear and she knew she was attracting the attention of those around her.

"Mom…shhh…" Bruce looked around and then suddenly stood to his feet. "Come on, let's go for a walk." Once outside, he rushed her around the corner and towards a small park near the elementary school.

"Bruce, tell me! You're sick, aren't you?"

Bruce nodded, "I am, Mama. It's bad. I…I have AIDS. I've had it for a long time. The doctors have done a lot for me over the years, but it's… it's bad, Mama. It's real bad."

The sobs that found their way to the surface were low and guttural. They came from the very core of her hopeless spirit. Caring little for her surroundings, she fell into his arms and once again cried the cries of a broken heart. "Noooo…nooooo!" she shouted over and over again. "Not my sons! You can't take both my sons!"

Barbara stumbled through the next eighteen months taking Bruce to his doctor appointments during the day, grieving David's death late into the night and dreading Eric's sermons on the weekends.

"Many will be deceived in the last days!" he shouted out one Sunday. "If you think it's bad now – *just wait*! It's only going to get worse!"

Barbara wanted to scream at him to stop. To just *shut up* for once! She needed something to encourage her. Something to give her joy! If God was a God of love, why had He placed her on this miserable earth only to live in a loveless marriage, bury her sons and dread the future? Was this all there was to being a Christian?

Oh, if only Jesus would come back and rescue them all from the endless pain!

By Tuesday afternoon of that week, Barbara was planning a second funeral. A late summer cold had taken its toll on Bruce's frail body. Rushing to the hospital, Barbara held his hand as her precious son closed his eyes for the last time.

Eric expected to preach the funeral service but, this time, Barbara put her foot down. "You despised my son in life. I'll not allow you to condemn him publicly in his death!"

Something changed in Eric's eyes and she knew she'd crossed the line. They made it through the well-meaning condolences and solemn funeral service with few words. When the door closed behind the last visitors in their home, Eric went to the basement and brought up two suitcases.

She heard him packing late into the night.

How had it come to this? They'd just celebrated their thirty-seventh anniversary! They'd served God together. They'd done their best to raise their sons in a Christian home! Was this the way He planned to repay them for all they'd done?

Sinking deeper into the covers of the bed she once shared with Eric, Barbara cried herself to sleep.

***

Hopelessness – it consumes the soul of so many Christians today… and it clings tightly to the Orphan Spirit.

Knowing only loneliness and despair, the Orphan Spirit finds little reason to hope. They have experienced only poverty, abandonment and insecurity their whole life and they doubt it will ever change.

A friend of ours traveled to Haiti soon after the devastating earthquake in 2010. Joel's compassion for the people, and their desperate situation, was evident. The photos he took helped prove his point that these were a people in need of hope.

One picture in particular so struck me that I asked for a copy of it - a copy that I hung by my desk and look at often. It's a picture of a young Haitian boy sitting on a rooftop, staring over the despair below. Joel told us that the boy never smiled – though Joel tried often to change that.

What was his story, I wondered? Where was his family? Missing? Dead? What had his life been like before January 12, 2010?

What were his thoughts, as he'd sit there each day, saying nothing... only staring at devastation?

When I consider the Hopeless Spirit of the Orphan, this is the picture I get. One who is left motionless by the tragedies of their past and sees nothing worth anticipating in the future.

Though taken into the Kingdom, the Orphan Spirit struggles to shed that blanket of hopelessness. The sorrow, brokenness and despair has been a part of who they are for so long, they don't know how to feel hope again. Or perhaps, they are afraid to feel hope again. After all, they lost everything before, what if it happens again? The only hope they know is to beg Jesus to Rapture His church.

The sad truth is, the Western Church is so accustomed to an escapism mentality that many see little reason to invest into future generations. Example? Children's ministry – find me a church that is turning people away from volunteering in children's ministry due to an overabundance of workers and I'll show you a church that is hope-filled. Once the body of Christ catches the vision of who our children are in the Kingdom, we won't be able to shake people away with a stick.

Barbara's gardening habits may seem silly to some but it reflects the hearts of so many within the Kingdom today.

Why bother?

The world is falling apart.

It's all gonna burn anyway.

What's the point?

But what are we leaving for our children and our children's children if we don't invest in their future? We cannot afford to live with an escapism mentality or we will have nothing to give to the next generation.

The Spirit of Hopelessness is not of God. He saw us, in our hopeless condition, and chose to take us off that rooftop overlooking despair. He chose to give us a future. He chose to give us a reason to hope.

But He didn't bring us in and leave us destitute and unprotected at the door. No, our Abba gave us access to all that He has. In fact, He even tells us in Romans 8 that the same Spirit that raised

Christ from the dead lives in us – and that Spirit brings us reasons to hope as well!

Satan has convinced us that we are on the defense, that he has more power than the sons and daughters of God – but he's wrong. The death of Jesus changed everything in that He now holds all power and authority – and He gives us access to it as well!

Jesus, Himself, tells us in Matthew 28 the most beautiful words for the hopeless Christian. He says, *"All authority has been given to Me in Heaven and on Earth."* NASB

Did you catch that? All...*all* authority!

How much authority?

All!

Webster's dictionary defines the word "all" this way - the whole, entire, total amount, quantity, or extent of. So if "all" is the sum total of how much authority Jesus has in Heaven and on Earth, then how much authority does that leave Satan to possess in Heaven and on Earth?

None.

He has none. He has only one thing– his mouth. And he uses it with no restraint. First, he uses his mouth to deceive the child of God. He even uses Scripture to do so – remember when he was tempting Jesus in the wilderness?

Second, Satan tries to fill our minds with doubt – "did God really say?" "Is God able to be trusted?"

Satan is amazing at discouraging people. He looks at the difficulties in our lives and keeps them shoved up in our face so that we are unable to see beyond the bleh in order to see the goodness of God.

The devil diverts the child of God as well. He seeks to pull our attention away from the gifts God is giving us and attempts to make other things appear more inviting. How many times people find themselves in an affair – thinking nothing could compare to a love like this – when ultimately, it only leads to a lifetime of heartache and regret.

Defeat is another of Satan's tactics. Once we fall for his attempts to deceive, discourage or divert us, the enemy is sure to be there to rub it in our face, letting us know what a complete failure we are.

And finally, the Devil delays us. He keeps us so busy with seemingly important tasks in order to keep us from what God really has in mind for us. Oftentimes, those tasks are good things, but are they things of God? Or simply busy work brought to us by Satan himself?

Why are we so afraid of the devil? Have you ever stopped to consider what might happen in your life if you gave as much credit to the power of God as you do to the devil?

What would happen if we as Believers took on a new mentality? What if, instead of fearing Satan's next move, we start living in such a way that Satan fears our next move? What if we stopped living as an orphan – dependent only on our own resources and instead rely on all that our Father has for us?

Truth is, the devil will only have as much power in your life as what you give him access to. He loves to come and tell you that you're not enough... too weak... too imperfect...too whatever. He's hoping his badgering will convince God's sons and daughters to open the door of their minds and let him have free reign with their brain...and often it works.

The Hopeless Spirit has it backwards. We are not defenseless, hopeless, powerless, feeble Christians! Acts 1:8 tell the words of Jesus when He promises that we will "receive power after the Holy Ghost has come up on you." What does it look like to live with power? With authority? The orphan has never experienced this phenomenon and the idea is foreign to him.

Power?

Authority?

"But the devil is roaming to and fro throughout the earth! Many will be deceived. It's only going to get worse!" you say. "Just look at Barbara's life! Could it have gotten any worse?"

Barbara did live a tough life, but it wouldn't have had to be hopeless. I know this because I saw a similar life lived out through the life of my Grandma Miller.

Grandma knew tragedy. She'd lost her firstborn son, Marvin, in a tractor accident when he was nine. Her birthday that year was spent watching her son's casket being lowered into the ground.

Years passed, and her heart was broken yet again when another son, my uncle Sheldon, admitted he was gay...and HIV positive. How is a conservative-minded pastor's wife in the 80's supposed to deal with this kind of news? The family (and there are lots...

and lots of us) had to each choose their individual reaction to Sheldon's news.

Some were sad.

Some were mad.

Some ignored him.

Some were ashamed of him.

Being just a kid myself, my personal response to my uncle was based on what I saw the rest of the family modeling. Feeling much confusion, I decided to ignore him and pretend he didn't exist... which wasn't hard since he lived across the country.

For years, I kept his existence a secret among my friends – after all, no one else had a gay uncle and I wasn't quite sure what to do with him. I watched from a distance as he was dishonorably discharged from the Marines, tsk tsking over the choices he had made.

When fellow believers eventually learned my family secret (after all, how does one keep such fantastic gossip under wraps forever and ever amen?), they were intrigued. Many wanted to see him –no, not meet him – just *see* him. After all, what does a gay uncle look like?

The words spoken were unkind. His life, mocked. His existence, ignored. Yet through all of Sheldon's life, I watched my deeply religious Grandma choose something completely contrary to what those around her suggested...or even approved of – she chose love.

Our family Thanksgiving meals were shared with both Sheldon and his partner. Both men were treated with love, dignity and respect. Grandma modeled for us all what it looks like to love someone – whether you agree with their life choices or not.

Grandma had lost one son to death. She knew the pain of separation – and I saw her combat the very thing that Satan was trying to use to remove another son from her life by simply choosing love.

Had she succumbed to her feelings on the matter, she would have affected not only Sheldon's life, but the lives of her ten remaining children, dozens of grandchildren and the generations following them. Why? Because we saw in Grandma an unwillingness to cave to hopelessness.

Did she agree with Sheldon's choices? No. But she looked beyond that and saw the man inside. The man who deserved just as much love as the next. The man who had been cast away by society, rejected by many and accused by the masses.

Religion told her to join them... but Jesus called her to love him.

Grandma's choices changed me. And I was able to put aside my pious condemnation towards my uncle before his death.

The Orphan Spirit struggles to see beyond the brokenness around them. Sons and daughters see the brokenness, yes, but they know their Father God is one who takes brokenness and restores it to something beautiful. Knowing this, they love unconditionally and invite those without hope to come to Jesus.

Consider this – what does condemning "sinners" benefit the child of God?

Suppose my Grandma had rejected her son…pushed him away… told him to change or he couldn't be a part of the family? Would he have changed his lifestyle?

No. Probably not.

And even if that approach had worked – suppose he would have changed his way of life to fit our preferences over his own – would changing his actions have changed his heart?

Again – probably not.

Here's my point – as a society, we look to the laws of the land as our definition of morality – and I won't deny that it has its place… but the laws of the land don't change people's hearts. If that were the case, our prisons would be empty! In the same way, the church can try to force their "laws" on people but that alone will never change hearts. It just won't.

Only the love and acceptance of the Father's heart towards the broken and hurting can bring change. To approach our culture the way Eric did – with pious condemnation, will never work. It is only a seedbed for hopelessness and people are sick of it. There is a world out there searching for a reason to get up in the morning. They're searching for a reason to dream again! The Kingdom offers that!

Acts 2 says, "in the last days… I (God) will pour out My Spirit on every kind of people…

Your young men will see visions, your old men dream dreams."

Vision!

Dreams!

People without hope have no vision – they have nothing to dream about. To live in hopelessness is not God's plan. My personal prayer has become that Abba Father would allow me the privilege of living life the way He envisioned for His people. I want full access to all the He originally planned. I don't want the lies of the devil, the opinions of people or the distractions of media to keep me from experiencing what it's like to live with the hope God intended for me from the beginning.

I want all the peace He has allotted for me.

I want to enjoy all the love He wants to plant in my heart for others.

I want to experience the courage He budgeted out for me.

I want to possess all the power He'd like to give me.

I want the faith He wants me to have.

My greatest curiosity wrapped up in holy fear and wonder is if I'll be able to look back over my life one day and see all that I missed because of hopelessness, doubt and fear.

What about you?

Are you like Joel's little Haitian buddy? Sitting on the balcony of desolation – surveying all that is lost and unable to envision a better day?

That's not Kingdom living. The Spirit of Hopelessness can be broken. You are a child of God – it's time to leave your post on

the roof and go out into the ruined cities and be a catalyst of hope
for those bound in despair.

> *The Spirit of the Sovereign LORD is on me,*
> *because the LORD has anointed me*
> *to proclaim good news to the poor.*
>
> *He has sent me to bind up the brokenhearted,*
> *to proclaim freedom for the captives*
> *and release from darkness for the prisoners*
> *to proclaim the year of the LORD's favor*
> *and the day of vengeance of our God,*
> *to comfort all who mourn,*
> *and provide for those who grieve in Zion—*
> *to bestow on them a crown of beauty*
> *instead of ashes,*
> *the oil of joy*
> *instead of mourning,*
> *and a garment of praise*
> *instead of a spirit of despair.*
> Isaiah 61:1-7 NIV

CHAPTER 12
SPIRIT OF PRIDE

Carol struggled to keep her ears tuned into the Sunday morning message.

She had plans. Big plans.

She could feel it in her bones. A calling. Something on the horizon.

Something big.

She couldn't say she knew exactly what it was but it didn't sway her conviction that God had something special for her.

Why else would He give her such a love for music and teaching? Even now she was preparing for a Bible Study she would be leading among the ladies of the church through the coming months. There was little more satisfying to her than to teach the Holy Word of God to her fellow sisters in the Lord.

And then there was Adam. Carol knew she had made quite the catch the day she gave him a ring and took his name. He was such a likable person and she knew he would make an amazing leader in the church one day.

Even now, the elder board seemed to see something special in Adam. Why, just last month, they had asked him if he might consider becoming an usher as they were in need of more "member care" on Sunday mornings.

To say the least, Adam and Carol were both slightly surprised and disappointed by the request – surprised that they would waste a fine leader like Adam on the simple task of ushering folks, and disappointed... well, disappointed for the very same reason. Adam was simply too valuable to give up his time helping in the back.

Perhaps the elders didn't realize that now. Or perhaps they just didn't care... or perhaps...perhaps they too saw the potential in Adam and feared giving him the chance to shine – knowing he would likely outshine them all.

That had to be it!

Adam and Carol hadn't wanted to think ill of the Elder board, but what other reason was there for asking him to take on such a lowly position? Carol consoled Adam and together the two determined that they would politely decline the request. They wanted Adam to remain available for service when the time came. If he committed to the Usher Team, he'd likely miss his next opportunity.

No. The answer was simple. He would not join the Usher Team. In the meantime, Adam and Carol would commit to praying for the pride they saw lurking somewhere in the lives of their church leaders.

It was a disappointment to say the least – seeing the weaknesses of these men whom they had so admired, but Adam and Carol reminded themselves that the elders were human too and imperfections were sure to arise from time to time.

They hadn't regretted their decision – and the ability to come and go without commitments or responsibilities each Sunday was nice too.

The service ended and Carol left Adam's side to go visit the ladies room.

"Carol!"

Carol turned to see Judith coming towards her.

"Hi Judith," Carol smiled at the lovely woman. Judith and her husband were the Worship Leaders here at Mount Bethel Fellowship. Carol had often envied Judith's talents and position in the church.

"You know, I'm so happy to see you," Judith reached out to give her a quick hug. "I was just thinking about you this very week!"

"Here it comes!" Carol stilled her thoughts as she waited for Judith to go on.

"I know you are such a busy woman, and, well, I just hate to ask, but..." Judith stammered as though searching for the right words.

"Oh Judith, I'd love to serve in *any* way I can! You know I would! What can I help you with?"

Would she be given a praise team of her own to lead? Probably not right away. On the other hand, she had stood behind Judith recently at a women's meeting and she was sure to sing loudly enough in Judith's direction so Judith would be able to hear her clear, soprano voice. Maybe that had paid off.

"Oh Carol, you're such a servant. I so appreciate that about you! The children's ministry is desperately searching for volunteers on Sunday mornings. Are you really certain you'd be able to help in any way you can?"

Carol gulped hoping her jaw had remained closed in light of this sudden change of direction.

Children's ministry?

How many ways can you say 'yuck'?

No! Eww!

Definitely not!

Sticky hands… snotty noses…whining…

VOMIT!

No! Judith couldn't be serious, could she?

"I'll let them know that you're available. Be sure to stop by the church office to fill out a volunteer form and pick up a schedule. I know the leadership will be so thankful for your willing spirit." Judith gave Carol one more quick hug before rushing down the hall.

Carol stood staring at the wall. Still in shock.

Children's ministry?

How did this happen?

The following Sunday, there she was, sitting on a too-small chair in the middle of a crowded classroom. Children clamored for attention, and though kind to them, Carol could only muster up the occasional smile as she simply went through the motions… all the while keeping an eye on the clock.

As soon as service was over and the last child had been checked out, Carol grabbed her coat and left the room. Snacks still littered the table and toys covered the floor but she didn't care. She hadn't wanted to do this in the first place.

It wasn't her passion!

It wasn't her calling!

"I'm exhausted!" Carol excused herself. *"I put my time in… and after all, what do they pay the janitors for anyway?"*

***

Children struggle to enjoy doing their chores whether an orphan or an heir, but a difference begins to emerge when a child begins to take ownership within their home.

Oftentimes, I will ask my own children to complete a simple household task and their lack of enthusiasm is less than stellar. As their parent, I am trying to instill in them an understanding that no matter the job, you can *choose* to do it with joy.

In the Kingdom, the Orphan Spirit refuses to take part in "home care" because they haven't taken ownership yet. To them, it is still a competition to try to find status and notoriety.

Their need for approval is crippling and it is often their Spirit of Pride that gets in the way of true servanthood. When asked to do something the Orphan Spirit considers beneath them, they will struggle to do the job well – oftentimes slopping through the job leaving those around them wishing they had just done it themselves.

Worse yet is the response of the orphan spirit when another is given a promotion within the Kingdom.

Carol and Adam will likely struggle to celebrate with their brothers and sisters when one of them is invited to join the Worship Team or Elder Board. Unfortunately, any friendships they may have are likely to end should their friend be the one to receive the promotion instead of them.

Inside the orphan mindset is the belief that anything you get is one less thing available to me, while sons and daughters recognize that they have access to all of the Father's resources.

Did Abba Daddy give you something special? Yay! Kingdom siblings celebrate with you because, though you got something good when they didn't, they still know they are loved! Your blessing is not a threat to those who have been adopted because the Kingdom mindset sees your gifts, your blessings, your promotions as a reminder of how giving the Father is and that He loves to give good gifts to His children.

Can the Orphan Spirit serve with joy? Absolutely! As long as it's the job they wanted.

Carol often dreamt of the ways in which she wanted to serve. Adam, too, desired a position of service in the church - their problem rested in the fact that they were unwilling to serve in *any* way they could. Instead, they desired positions within the church that would provide them with a sense of significance.

This type of serving is not service done for the King. On the contrary, it is self-serving. The only person the Orphan Spirit seeks to serve is himself.

The Orphan Spirit longs for status among their peers. For so long, they lived as one without a name...without a place in this world... without purpose or value. Because of this desire for status, they have little value for the weak. If you are unable to promote the Orphan Spirit in anyway, you have no worth to them.

Though brought into the Kingdom, the drive for acknowledgment is consuming and overpowering and often the orphan refuses to serve the least of these. When "roped" into a job they didn't want, they point out with regularity that they just don't "have a passion for it" or that they "aren't called to do this" and they search for the nearest exit. In the meantime, they pout while they work, complain often, perform sloppily and show little respect towards those they are serving.

This is a curious characteristic because, at the same time, the orphan has a crippling need for approval. So why wouldn't they seek to serve in any capacity?

The janitor at my home church is a wonderful example of one who has the heart of a son who desires to serve his Father.

Elden was one of the founding members of our church. Most would consider themselves deserving of lofty titles and numerous accolades, yet he, along with his wife, Cindy, can be found serving in various ways around the church. It is nothing unusual to see Cindy washing a window or Elden gathering up trash.

Elden spends countless hours – quite likely more than anyone realizes, working at the church, and doing a wonderful job of keeping it clean.

One evening, I noticed Elden cleaning in the foyer after youth group. "Elden, I am so sorry for the mess these kids are making!" I apologized. "You probably had cleaned in here before we came tonight!"

"Don't apologize for that!" Elden was adamant, "A messy church is a sign that there is life happening. If I didn't have any dirt or trash to clean up, that would mean there was nothing happening around here."

I was speechless.

His attitude astounded me! I was humbled, inspired and convicted.

I've noticed something about Elden since that day – he does jobs that few would be willing to do. On top of that, he is always ready with a smile and a kind word, never complaining and eager to serve.

His work gets little praise. It is seldom publicly acknowledged, few take time to thank him for his endless service…but still, he shows up. He grabs the vacuum, he scrubs the toilets and he mops the floors…and he does it with joy!

It is only as the orphan recognizes their place in the Kingdom that a sense of gratitude will stir their hearts towards service. Sons and daughters are bursting with joy for all their Abba Daddy has done and in their desire to bring Him joy, they care little for what He asks of them – they only seek to please Him and bring Him joy whether promoted and praised… or simply called to serve, like Elden, in humble solitude.

CHAPTER 13
THE SPIRIT OF SHAME

He sat staring across the vast expanse nighttime sky. Yellow stars poked holes in the darkness along with the occasional red blinking light of an airplane.

"The firmament showeth His handiwork." The familiar Scripture scrolled through Jeremy's mind followed by another. "What is man that thou art mindful of him?"

Jeremy wondered at the verses he'd learned as a child. *Yes, who am I? That God would be mindful of me?* Jeremy pushed out a puff of air, the thought was preposterous. The only thoughts God might have of him were 101 ways to throw him into the lake of fire.

No, God would not be 'mindful' of Jeremy. Not if He was the God Jeremy's mother proclaimed Him to be.

He'd grown up going to church every Sunday with his parents and older brother. His older brother had made his parents proud – headed for the mission field straight out of high school. While there, Steven had felt the call of God on his life to go to Africa. After his internship was done in Belize, Steven had gotten a doctorate in Language and Cross-Cultural Studies at Southern Kansas Theological Seminary. There, he met his wife Karen. The two had graduated, packed up what little they could carry, gave the rest away and bought one-way tickets to Uganda.

While Steven had been busy applying for sainthood, Jeremy had been sowing his wild oats. Oh, he'd tried to follow in his brother's footsteps. He wanted to be a good kid. Make his parents proud. But he wasn't cut out for the mission field.

"That's fine, Jeremy," his mother had assured him. "Just be who God called *you* to be." Jeremy had nodded but still couldn't help feeling as though he'd never measure up.

He finished school, got a job at a local baseball facility, The Bullpen, and decided to take a year to decide on his major. His dream was to make it to the big leagues, but he knew the odds were stacked against him.

That year turned into two and Jeremy's mom worried about him. "Are you coming to church this Sunday, honey?"

"Sorry, Ma. I promised I'd pick up an extra shift this weekend."

She didn't say anything. Didn't have to. He could read her mind. He knew her concerns about his lack of interest in church, college and 'a real job'. Jeremy shrugged. He didn't much care what her or dad thought. He wasn't Steven and the more she pushed him to be like him, the less Jeremy felt willing to comply.

The following year was tough. Jeremy's dad fell ill. Cancer. Fourth Stage Melanoma. Jeremy felt like he'd been punched in the gut.

That Sunday found him sitting in the pews next to his parents. The pastor called them forward and prayed a special prayer over their family – spending extra time begging God to 'work a miracle in Larry's body'.

Jeremy waited until he was in the privacy of his basement bedroom, then he too prayed. Prayed like he'd never prayed before. Tears streaming down his face he begged God to have mercy on his father. Pleaded with him to spare his life.

His dad was everything to him. His rock. His hero. Jeremy was barely twenty, for crying out loud. He couldn't live life without his father yet. Not even close!

Four months later, Jeremy stood next to his mother at the mouth of an open grave. The wind whipped up clouds of dust in the Kansas heat as he listened to the words of the pastor attempting to offer comfort to the bereaved.

Ashes to ashes.

Dust to dust.

Jeremy went into auto-pilot. Get through this and then get out of here. He was done. Done with it all! Done with this stupid religious junk. Done praying to a God who obviously didn't care. Done!

He faked his way through the meal following the graveside service, annoyed that people could so quickly return to somber smiles and quiet chatter about everyday life over plates of potato salad and apple pie while his own world lay dead in the grave two hundred yards behind the church.

If there really was a God, He was a sorry excuse for a God. And He certainly wasn't one Jeremy was willing to stake his life on.

Jeremy took his mother home, kissed her good-bye and drove away.

**

After leaving Kansas, he'd made his way to the Florida Keys where he found a job as a bartender near the beach. It wasn't long before the alcohol he served became the best friend he'd ever known.

Throwing out every conviction he'd held, he dove headlong into the life of sin his brother was across the ocean attempting to save people from.

The years passed by in a fog. Jeremy might not have been good at being a Christian but he made an excellent sinner. The alcohol helped fight off the sorrow he carried over the loss of his father, but soon the pain was accompanied by guilt and shame over the hurt his choices would surely have caused the man he now grieved. It wasn't long before the alcohol was no longer enough.

Jeremy added drugs to the mix… as well as any woman who was interested.

His mother's prayers were answered when eight years after he'd walked away, Jeremy found himself at the altar of a little church.

It was September 11, 2001. The day the world changed.

He'd stood in front of his TV and watched the smoke climb up into the piercing blue sky and he knew he couldn't live another day in this sick twisted world without God.

In repentance, he told God how sorry he was for all he had done and begged for a second chance. God granted Jeremy that forgiveness and Jeremy walked out of that little chapel a new man.

He could feel it in his soul.

Packing his bags, he said good-bye to Florida and moved back home to be near his mother. He felt a burning desire to make restitution for all the pain he'd caused her. Once home, Jeremy got involved in his mother's church. The shame of his past had followed him and he willingly served selflessly in an effort to show God how sorry he was.

By 2003, Jeremy's life had changed drastically. Now married, he counted himself fortunate for all the blessings God had given him: a beautiful home, loving wife and a baby on the way.

But late at night, he'd felt a familiar shame crawl into his room and envelop his being.

What kind of jerk was he? Leaving his mom like he did? Becoming an alcoholic? Druggie? He was so unworthy of all these things. He didn't deserve it.

Steven deserved good things but not Jeremy.

Never Jeremy.

The shame and guilt consumed him and he longed to be free from his inner struggle. By the time baby Jack was born, Jeremy had a deep dark secret.

He was drinking again.

He tried to keep it on the down low. Distracted with the arrival of the baby, Jackie didn't seem to notice what was happening with her husband.

The day she discovered it was *not* a good day.

If Jeremy felt guilty before, his shame reached new heights as he begged for forgiveness. Jackie agreed to counseling but the light in her eyes was gone.

Ashamed, Jeremy spent more hours at work, hoping to show her he was a faithful husband and provider. The larger paychecks didn't please her and the chasm between them widened.

Jeremy continued to work longer hours but now his reasons were two-fold. It kept him away from his nagging wife…and it gave him more time alone with his computer.

He knew he shouldn't be looking at porn, but what could he say? He was a lonely man. A lonely man with needs.

Driving home each night, Jeremy would beg God to forgive him, to help him be the man he knew he should be. But nothing changed. He continued to sneak a trip to the bar every chance he could, and now he had the ease of pornography at his fingertips when he got his first smartphone.

The battle was raging… and Jeremy knew he was losing.

He pulled into the driveway of his home late one night, knowing he couldn't go on like this. But what choice did he have? He had tried to be the child of God he knew he should be. He wanted the abundant life he'd read about in the Book of John, but how could he, Jeremy, ever accept a gift of that magnitude?

He was the worst of all sinners! The lowest of the low - at least in his eyes. And perhaps in the eyes of some of his fellow church members. He'd seen the condemnation in their eyes. He knew what they were thinking.

He stared at the nighttime sky, wondering at a God his mother said wanted to be his Father. How he wished he was worthy to be called a son.

Steven was worthy. So worthy. But not Jeremy. Never Jeremy.

Shoving a glass bottle in the trashcan beside the garage, Jeremy hung his head in defeat and walked into the house.

***

How many Kingdom kids are living much like Jeremy?

They don't measure up.

Can't compete.

Don't belong.

What kind of Abba Father would want someone like them? Someone who has failed time and time and time again.

The Orphan Spirit clings to his box of unworthiness. He is forever reminded of where he came from and is unable to let of his past. He is able to go through the motions for a time, but carrying the baggage of shame wears him out and trips him up.

His guilt refuses to let him lay his shame at the feet of the Father and accept the gift of complete liberty to run free and unhindered throughout the Kingdom.

Consider if you were to adopt a child. Suppose as you brought him into your home you would begin dreaming of all the things you want your child to do. "Here's a swing set, buddy. I built it for you! There's a fort up top, a slide and even this awesome rock wall!"

Your son looks it over with both desire and joy – maybe even climbs up on it for a little, but soon, he comes looking for you again. "Hi Dad."

"Hey son. Are you done playing already?"

"I like it, dad. I just... I just don't think I better play on it."

Your heart sinks. Doesn't he like it? "Is there something wrong with the swing set?"

"No, dad. I love it... it's just... well."

"What is it, bud? You can tell me anything."

"I just... I don't think I deserve it, daddy. I mean. Remember, I'm not really your kid. You probably don't really even want a kid like me. I mean, who would want me?"

Your heart sinks, wondering what you can say or do to reassure your son that you do love him... you do want him.

"Buddy, no! You *are* mine! I love *you*! I *chose* you!! I gave up everything so I could call you mine!"

Reassured, your son runs off to play again, but soon, he's back. "I'm not good enough." A little later... "You wouldn't want me. I'm not good enough. I'm too short...I can't even play with it right. I fell down. I got hurt..."

On and on and on come the constant attempts to convince you that he is unlovable.

What feelings would that conjure up in a parent? This is your child – the one you moved heaven and earth to bring home. You gave up countless hours and resources. Dreamed of this day. Moved beyond your comfort zone. Let the world see your greatest vulnerabilities in order to make his world right...in order to bring him home...and *he... doubts... your... love*?

What more would you need to do?

The correlation is too beautiful to pass up.

It exposes a love that is deep... too deep for words to describe... and a rejection that cuts to the core...leaving your parent heart wounded and raw...and longing.

What more could Abba Daddy do to prove to you that He simply wants you?

Not based on anything you've done – but because being your Daddy is everything He's ever wanted.

When the Orphan Spirit refuses God's love, he is, in essence, saying God is incapable of *ever* doing *enough* to prove His love to you.

***

Again, imagine you adopted a child and one day you discovered your little girl had taken a black marker and colored all over your newly remodeled living room walls. On top of that frustration, she'd also used a hammer to pound some holes in the drywall.

Double grr!

Your frustration level is at an all time high, and you both know there will be consequences. You're aggravated, she's ashamed… tears are streaming… but, here's the question.

Is she still your daughter?

Does the adoption survive her discretions? Would you still choose to be her mommy in spite of what she's done?

God the Father's love for His children stands in spite of what we do. And it's when the orphan sees how perfectly loved they are by Him, they feel secure enough to stop fighting Him – to stop entertaining the fear that He'll change His mind.

Sons and daughters know this is their Forever Daddy and there's nothing they can do to stop His love. Does that make them find a marker for the nearest living room wall?

No!

Rather, it sends them looking for Abba.

"Hold me, Papa."

"I love You, Abba."

"Will You spend time with me? Talk to me?"

"Can I get You a drink?"

The son doesn't gift his Father with acts of service out of guilt for his past –

NO! Instead, he searches his Father's Kingdom for ways that he can help his Abba Daddy.

Sadly, the shame-filled orphan often falls back into his old patterns because of his orphan siblings. When Proud Orphan sees Shame Orphan coming out of his shell, Pride is quick to remind Shame of his past – " you have no right! Look where you came from! Look what you did!"

Broken, the shame-filled orphan agrees, and returns to pit of despair, never believing he is worth the price that was paid for his adoption.

So what do we do?
Keep on sinning
so God can keep on forgiving?
I should hope not!
Romans 6:1 MSG

CHAPTER 14
THE ORPHAN SPIRIT

There are countless ways the Orphan Spirit could be illustrated. Stories we see, hear and experience every single day within the walls of our churches.

Living in a society that is self-centered, self-entitled and self-absorbed doesn't help. As we've seen throughout this book, an orphan is one who is unsettled – never knowing what tomorrow holds. He must white-knuckle his way through life, clinging to anything that offers a measure of security.

A life of uncertainty leaving one struggling to think about anyone other than themselves – this is the Orphan Spirit.

She is afraid... dependent on her own strength. While she appears confident, inwardly, she knows her weaknesses and it scares the mess out of her. What if someone finds out? What if she fails? What if someone is better than her? Gets more than her? Loved more than her?

Her fear plays out in a variety of ways – bold, outspoken and obnoxious. She holds an air of "I'll get you before you get me" and accuses people of not liking her.

Then there's the quiet orphan in the corner, hoping she'll go unnoticed. She looks around the Kingdom, wondering where she'll fit in – and if she'll fit in at all. Intrigued by the loud orphan, she'll cling to her – seeing her as a form of safety and security. The loud orphan sees the quiet one as an object to control – thus both are satisfied in their needs.

The problem is – both feed into the other's weakness and unless freed from their orphan mindset, they are likely to be the church gossips....often becoming the source for church drama and dissension. Their fear drives them to throw others under the bus, caring little for the pain they cause to their brothers and sisters.

Orphans without a family – a home – a name, long for identity. They want to know they matter to someone. That they have value.

Those with the Orphan Spirit are hungry for status. They need to know they have worth. The orphan begins to look at people as a means to an end. Caring little about the other person, they only see them as a rung in their ladder.

We saw this with Teresa going to see Sister Pam. Did she really care about Pam? No. She wasn't even in her room more than five minutes! She knew she could get away with a quick visit and no one would know the difference. Pam wouldn't know, the Pastor's wife wouldn't know, Kenzie wouldn't care… and Teresa's ego was fed by the response she got on Facebook.

Pam was a rung in Teresa's ladder… and she didn't even know it.

Those who are fighting their way to the top are so focused on value; they are shameless in their actions. Using brothers and sisters to achieve personal goals, they are often unable to empathize with another's pain. So accustomed are they to watching out for themselves, they walk over others – needing to survive at any cost and often leave a trail of brokenhearted victims in their wake.

Self-centered, the Orphan Spirit repels those who are considered to be "the least of these" – which includes children. She prefers only the company of those who admire her and can promote her in some way. She delights in discovering the failures of others and is quick to point out those faults to anyone who will listen. At the same time, she is unwilling to accept responsibility for her own actions. Saying she's sorry is difficult.

A daughter of Christ has discovered that focusing on God compels you to love others without reservation. She recognizes that loving on others is in essence, loving on God. She takes pleasure in promoting encouraging truths and always looks for the best in another. She admits when she's been wrong and grants others the privilege of offering forgiveness.

As a mother, fewer things wear me out more than dealing with sibling rivalry. My kids know they are loved and adored – but inevitably, the question still comes at me from time to time.

"Why did you let him do this and not me?" Etc, etc.

Grrrr!! What does the kid expect me to say? "Because he's my favorite child?" Ha! Of course not! I would never say that! Parents don't have favorites! (If they do, they need some counseling.)

That beautiful moment when each of my children entered the world, I fell deeply, passionately, fiercely in love. There is *nothing* I wouldn't do to protect my kids. I don't value or cherish one over the other, nor do I give one more than another.

But my kids don't always see it that way.

Kingdom orphans struggle with sibling rivalry too. Remember Dana and Becca? Dana was eaten up with jealousy over the admiration Becca was receiving for making the signs for the ladies. Teresa also was annoyed that Heather would be getting the accolades for planning the Women's Conference.

What they fail to realize is that their Father has endless resources. Did your sister get a new car? Bigger house? Job promotion? Yay! You should rejoice! Why? Because it is a reminder to you that you both have a Father who delights in giving good gifts to His children.

Or perhaps your brother was given the church position you wanted or your sister was asked to lead a song you love. Kingdom kids rejoice with their siblings over the good things they get because they know there is no end to the goodness of their Abba. More for you does not mean less for me. That's not how the Kingdom works!

Inside the Palace, the gifts are abundant, endless and beautiful.

The Orphan Spirit needs to be in control. When uncertainties arise, he is prone to anger and fits of rage based mostly on the fact that he does not trust – since he was once abandoned and unloved, he believes in his heart that it can happen again and he is willing to manipulate situations in an effort to control his environment.

Sons and daughters rest secure because they know that their Abba Daddy has their lives in His hands.

The daughter of Christ is confident that she is loved – it is not an arrogance or pride.. it is simply confidence that she has been brought into the Kingdom. She is no longer an orphan but is in fact a child of the King.

When studying the Orphan Spirit, it's easy to identify friends and acquaintances with various Orphan Spirit tendencies, yet my prayer for each reader would be that we could all take a long, hard look at our own lives and consider where we might see glimpse of the Orphan Spirit.

It is my opinion that as long as we live on planet Earth, we will never fully be released from the Orphan Spirit. The challenge is to continually pursue living as sons and daughters, but with little warning we can find ourselves with an orphan mentality in ways we hadn't noticed before.

Even as I write these words, conviction spears my heart and I am made aware of ways in which I too need to rely more fully on my Abba Daddy and it is my desire to be aware of my Father moment by moment...to release my desire for control into His capable hands...to return to His presence each time I stray...to discover what all is available to me as His daughter... and to daily pursue what Kingdom living really looks like.

CHAPTER 15
JONAH AND ESTHER SPIRITS

Jonah and Esther – two Bible characters you don't often see mentioned together, but they make an interesting correlation into the outcome of an Orphan mindset vs. Son & Daughters mindset.

Let's start with Jonah.

He was called by God to be a prophet. He probably did all the usual prophet-y things.

Wore prophet clothes, talked prophet talk, prayed prophet prayers… and lived as one would expect from a good and proper prophet.

The Bible doesn't give Jonah's opinion on his status but you can't help but wonder if he enjoyed his position in the Kingdom. Being known as the man of God is quite a title! Yes, there are responsibilities that go along with it, but there is no mention of Jonah having a problem performing…that is, until the day he was called to Ninevah.

God was fed up with the Ninevites and Jonah didn't blame him. How many times do we look down our religious noses, appalled at the sins of another. "Look at them, God! They're awful! Punish them for their wicked ways!"

God agreed that the Ninevites needed to be punished but, in typical God-like fashion, He wanted to offer mercy first.

"Jonah, I want you to go down there and tell them to repent." Jonah didn't think twice, he stood to his feet and headed as far away from Ninevah as he could go.

You know the story. Jonah ends up in a storm, which ultimately puts him in the belly of a great fish. There, Jonah cries out to God, God extends mercy to Jonah as well, and soon Jonah is heading to Ninevah.

Jonah cries "Repent," the Ninevites do just that and the whole city is saved.

Oh happy day!

Unless you're Jonah.

Jonah was ticked. "I knew it! I knew You would do that! That's why I ran to Tarshish! I knew You were sheer grace and mercy. I knew You weren't easily angered! I knew You'd love them and drop Your plans of punishment and come up with a program of forgiveness. I knew it!"

Jonah is so mad, he throws an unsightly temper tantrum – completely unfit for a prophet of God. "Fine – if You won't kill them then just kill me!"

God didn't. He allowed Jonah a time out under a makeshift shelter of leafy branches on the outskirts of town. God caused a broad-leafed tree to spring up. It grew over Jonah and cooled him off. This pleased Jonah and he began to think life wasn't so bad after all.

But then, God sent a worm and the tree was withered away by the next morning. On top of that, God decided to turn up the heat. The sun rose hot in the morning sky. Jonah was miserable! "Just kill me, God! I'm better off dead!"

God comes to Jonah, reprimanding him for his attitude and asks him this, "How is it that you change your feelings from pleasure to anger overnight about a mere shade tree that you did nothing to get? It was here one day and gone the next – without you even lifting a finger. So why can't I change my mind about Ninevah – this city of over 120,000 people?"

From the beginning of the story until the end, Jonah is all about number one. Even his prayer in the belly of the whale was focused on himself and his feelings.

Jonah doesn't care about the people *at all*! He wants nothing to do with them. He would have found great pleasure over seeing their city go up in flames. Even as he sat in the heat watching the city, hoping God would punish them, Jonah could only pout about his personal comfort.

Think about it. Really think about it – he's watching, waiting for judgment to fall on a city full of people. Hundreds and thousands of people! And as he waits to witness their destruction, he's whining about a lack of air conditioning.

Prophet or not, Jonah has an Orphan Spirit. He is self-centered, lacks mercy and is unable to sympathize with others. He is the perfect example of how "godly people" can still do the work of the Lord while carrying the Orphan Spirit.

I cringe when I stop to consider how easy it is to act like Jonah. An unfortunate amount of Christians today are called judgmental, critical and hateful – and, in some cases, rightfully so. That reputation comes from an unwillingness to offer love to the Ninevites in our lives. Too many tear apart the sinner while piously nodding their heads when judgment falls.

But what if God chooses mercy?

Whether He does or does not is His choice.

Our job is to love like Christ and obey His direction in our lives.

***

Next, let's take a look at an actual orphan. We know her as Esther but she is first introduced to us in the Bible as Hadassah.

After her parents died, Hadassah's Uncle Mordecai takes her into his own home. Life was good. She had a home and family. Uncle Mordecai even gave her a new name – Esther.

Some time went by when news hit the streets that the king was looking for a new wife. Esther soon found herself in the palace, waiting to see if she would be crowned queen.

While we look at the story of Esther with much admiration, we would likely have a different opinion if it were to happen today.

First, the king didn't like his wife, so he divorced her. Then, Esther spends a year prepping for a night with the king - a night that didn't include just dinner and movie if you know what I mean.

After spending the night, she must wait to hear if he liked her… after all, he had many women to choose from. Eventually, Esther is the one the king chooses and she becomes the queen.

What stands out to me, is this - when the time came that her people, the Jews, needed her to use her position inside the kingdom, Esther had a choice to make.

Perhaps she told herself she wasn't enough. She was, after all, a foreigner. She had humble beginnings. She was an orphan! She had seen what happened with wife number one and she stood to lose all that she had – she could end up back in the streets again – or dead.

Still, Esther used her position and stepped out in faith – and God was with her.

The body of Christ has a choice – we can be like Jonah, self-absorbed, entitled, unloving and angry – or we can recognize our position in the family of God and boldly step out and do what He's called us to do…even when the outcome is uncertain.

Both Jonah and Esther accomplished great things for God, but only one had the heart of a Kingdom Child while doing it.

CHAPTER 16
SPIRITUAL FATHERS & MOTHERS

To be an orphan simply means to be one who has no parents.

While we understand this in the natural realm, what does this look like in the spirit realm?

As we've seen throughout the stories in this book, orphans are ones who must watch out for themselves. While they foster a neediness on one hand, they also carry a strong sense of independence. Since they do not have parents of their own, they must parent themselves.

Parents are given to us to provide us with identity – we take their name and know where we belong. Parents offer us approval, they protect us, they promote us and they validate us. They see in us our giftings and abilities and they encourage us in those areas.

Orphans are left to fulfill these roles in their lives for themselves and when entering the Kingdom, they begin looking for a stage on which to display their abilities. Their independence pushes people away and they are left, once again, feeling alone and discouraged.

We live in a fatherless generation, which is why the Orphan Spirit runs so rampant throughout both our society and in our churches. This is not what God intended for His Kingdom. Malachi 4:5-6 ESV says,

> *"Behold, I will send you Elijah the prophet before*
> *the great and awesome day of the Lord comes.*
> *And he will turn the hearts of fathers to their children*
> *and the hearts of children to their fathers, lest I come and*
> *strike the land with a decree of utter destruction."*

God's desire is family, yet many believers have encountered abuse from parents, church leadership or other authority figures, thereby determining that no one is worthy of trust. They wander aimlessly, not realizing that what they are really looking for is a family.

God is the Ultimate Father. He is the Source of our identity, approval, security and promotion. But He went a step further by giving us Spiritual Fathers and Mothers within the local church.

This comes in various forms – obviously our pastors would fill that role but it can also be those who guide, encourage and lead in other capacities. The Orphan Spirit's job is to simply take on the role of a son or daughter. They must lay aside their independent spirit and allow themselves to be parented.

A couple of years ago, I saw this play out so plainly in the lives of two couples. These families had no connection to one another, yet their situations were ironically similar.

Both were struggling to save their marriages after one of the spouses from each marriage had had an affair. Both couples decided to go for marriage counseling. The first couple resented the guidance given to them and refused to see their own part in the breakdown of the marriage. The wife in particular had little respect for the advice given, and neither was willing to take part in the counselor's homework assignments between counseling sessions.. Each felt they knew all the answers – and that their spouse was the problem.

Eventually, the only thing this couple could agree on was that *both* the counselor and Pastor of their church were wrong. So they left.

Their marriage still struggles to this day, their lives are filled with bitterness and pain and they continue to move from church to church in their search for a place to belong.

The second couple came into the marriage counselor just as hurt… just as broken. They realized this was a last ditch effort to save their marriage.

The counselor gave them the same advice as he had the first couple. He offered the same homework and set aside the same amount of time as he had with the others. All efforts were the same on his part…but there was a difference.

The attitudes of the second couple were quite unlike the first.

This couple listened with a hunger, took note of their role in the problems they were now facing, spent time acknowledging their faults, respected their counselors time and efforts and did everything he advised them.

They looked to him and their church leadership as their spiritual fathers, and their lives made 180 degree turn. With a spirit of humility and a willingness to serve, they became established in their local church and within a short time were given key roles of leadership – roles they wouldn't have dreamed of a year earlier.

The difference simply comes through the Orphan's willingness to give up their independence and embrace the gift of a spiritual father and mother. Likewise, spiritual fathers and mothers must look at their role as a calling rather than a career.

They cannot base their success solely on the numbers, the programs, or the praise. Sometimes being a spiritual parent is hard...sometimes being a *parent* is hard... but parenting is a calling – not a career... - and trust me, there is little praise thrown around when parenting. ("Oh mother, I love when you clean the toilets! And you did an amazing job folding my laundry today!") But with a calling comes passion and focus for the lives of those in your care.

As a mother, I would never consider bigger and better options. These are my kids! I love them with all that I am – even on the days when they get on my ever-lovin' nerves – and I will be here for them in the good and in the bad. They are my calling, my passion and my focus in life – and they know that I'm here for them.

Are you a spiritual father or mother to someone? Have you been called to ministry? It's not always easy, is it? Trust me, I get it. Tim and I have been youth ministers for a seven of the seventeen years we've been married.

I'll admit – I didn't always want to do youth ministry, but God did a work in my heart and now we have a love for these teens that is unexpected and powerful. We've laughed with them, cried with them, prayed, played and worshipped together. They have our hearts – and Tim and I give them the same amount of love and attention no matter how many are sitting in our circle.

Do we always feel like getting off the couch to go to youth group on a Sunday evening? Do we always feel like making a schedule? Planning a trip? Dealing with drama? Not always... but those kids are our kids. And all that other stuff? That's just part of it. It's a calling God's given us and we've found that surrendering our will to His will bring greater blessing than ever imagined. And He doesn't leave us without resources. When days are hard, He reminds us to cast our burdens onto Him and He will sustain us. (Every time I've whined about missing a Sunday afternoon nap, I end up coming home from youth group with a heart overwhelmed by love for our teens.)

***

King David's life speaks into the heart of fatherhood – but not in the way one would think. Though David was called a man after God's own heart, he failed in many ways as a father. His family was in complete chaos because of his unwillingness to lead.

The first sign of trouble begins when his oldest son, Amnon, raped his half-sister, Tamar. King David heard about it but chose to look the other way. The injustice of it all was too much for David's other son, Absalom. For years, Absalom seethed with rage about the injustice until he eventually killed Amnon.

So David has rape and murder on his hands, but still...he does nothing.

Why? Why would he ignore this?

In the meantime, Absalom flees to another city where he stays for sometime. Eventually, the king allows Absalom to return home – as long as he promises to not show his face to his father.

This David is the very man we praised in the story of Mephibosheth. The one who took in his enemy's crippled grandson – gave him a place at his table. Could it be that we find it easier to serve those with whom we have no relationship? Could it be that we find it easier to give of our resources rather than our love?

In spite of their rocky relationship, David still had a deep love for Absalom. We see this when Absalom was killed and the king grieved deeply over the loss of his son.

I can't help but wonder what difference there might have been had David stepped in back when Tamar was first violated. What if he had brought correction and justice to the situation from the very beginning? Consider all the emotional turmoil, wasted years and lost relationships he would have saved his family if only he had chosen to be the father he should have been. His life goes to show that we can never fully shed the Orphan Spirit while in our human condition. It is something we will battle in various ways as long as we live on planet earth.

Inside the walls of the Kingdom, God has given us men and women to act as our spiritual fathers and mothers. How many are unable or unwilling to lead as they should? How many are looking the other way – choosing to ignore the issues as opposed to calling sin sin?

How much division and dissension could be avoided if pastors lead with courage, passion and confidence? Instead, in many churches, we have the tail wagging the dog. Pastors are unable to serve, protect, nurture and lead their church family as a father should due to a fear of offending key members and ultimately losing their jobs.

I am fortunate enough to find myself under a church leadership that presents a united front. Like any set of parents, I know they have their differences from time to time – but the family doesn't see it – nor do they have to deal with it.

While a pastor, in most cases, is paid for what he does, he also should be given the right to lead with confidence. Kids don't get to fire their parents and, while there are certainly cases where it is necessary to have a pastor step down, I can't help but wonder what our churches would look like if the fear of losing their jobs was taken away from a pastor.

We have bickering, gossip, backstabbing and selfishness filling our pews while sons and daughters sit unprotected in the midst of it. When spiritual fathers and mothers are unable or unwilling to step in and offer them the protection they need, the orphans inflict gaping wounds on those around them… and we stand scratching our heads trying to figure out why people leave?

But the responsibility doesn't lie solely on the leadership. Each person must also reflect on their own thoughts and actions.

Are they promoting self? Or one another?

Do they value teamwork? Or independence?

Do they respect their authorities? Or prefer to be in control?

Do they trust their leadership? Or are they quick to undermine?

Until we are able to leave our orphan identity at the door, we will never be able to fully embrace and enjoy all that God the Father has for us. Furthermore, the family of God will miss out on the joys, blessings and victories that come from being a loving and united family.

CHAPTER 17
THE SPIRITS OF ABSALOM AND JEZEBEL

There are two additional spirits that fall under the category of the Orphan Spirit – Absalom and Jezebel. The two are wreaking havoc throughout the Kingdom. I believe they must be exposed for who they are and what they are doing.

Let's recap their stories.

We talked about Absalom earlier. His father, King David, had failed to punish Absalom's older brother, Amnon, for raping their sister, Tamar.

In all honesty, I tend to feel sorry for the guy. His father was unwilling to bring justice to a terrible situation and Absalom let it consume him. The failings of the leadership in his life was unfortunate, but Absalom did not have the right to let another's faults dictate his actions.

But he did, and because of it, he led an angry, bitter life – which ultimately led to his early death.

Absalom's spirit lives on in our churches.

Consider how many have been hurt by the failures of those in leadership. What begins as great respect for pastors, elders and the like, can slowly give root to a tiny seed. Seeds of frustration, criticism and discontent.

"His sermons are so boring."

"The music is too loud."

"What were they thinking when they picked this carpet?"

Absalom spread doubt in the minds of his father's kingdom by second guessing David's leadership. In the same breath, he would paint a picture of what life might be like if he were in charge.

The Kingdom is filled with many who are exceptionally gifted people. Being gifted is wonderful, being anointed is better.

I'd choose listening to an anointed worship leader, pastor or teacher any day over one who is only naturally gifted in that area.

Are you gifted? Great! Does that make you more valuable than others in the Kingdom? Nope. Sorry to burst your bubble.

The one who recognizes where his gifts come from, surrenders it back to God, wanting only to use his abilities to point back to Jesus, is the one who will carry an anointing along with the gift.

Absalom may have made an exceptional leader for his country but the anointing was on David. Though offended by this same man, Absalom should have chosen to honor his leader and seek to promote the kingdom. Had he done so, his story would have ended much differently.

The Absalom spirit can be identified by one who carries an air of independence. He (or she –the Absalom and Jezebel spirits can rest on either gender) refuses to submit to those in authority over him and will begin to build a following of his own.

The Absalom Spirit wants to be recognized. He is all about self-promotion. Every action is done with the purpose of gaining praise and promotion. In 2 Samuel, we read about Absalom asking to go to Hebron to fulfill a vow he'd made to the Lord. He told King David that he wanted to go there to worship God.

Given permission, Absalom swung into action with a carefully planned goal of winning the hearts of the kingdom and being crowned king. He invited two hundred oblivious men along with him. Among them, he strategically placed secret agents who would begin proclaiming Absalom king at a precise moment.

Imagine it with me – the crowd is honored to have been noticed by this dynamic and handsome prince. He invites a select few – to accompany him on a special trip – and you're one of them! You stand there among the others watching him worship your God, and suddenly a trumpet blares. You look around, surprised and a voice cries out, "Absalom is king in Hebron!"

This is news to you but then another voice joins in the chant. Confused, you wonder if you missed the memo. The hype is contagious and you find yourself considering what it might be like to have a king such as this.

He is a prince after all.

And handsome!

And so eloquent and strong.

Without a second thought, you join in with the crowd, proclaiming the wonders of

Absalom – and in essence, defecting from your king.

In the Kingdom, the Absalom spirit still has the same plan. He wraps his strategies in a "spiritual covering" ("I'm going to Hebron to worship"). The unsuspecting get drawn in and become victims in a war they didn't plan to fight.

The stronger the Absalom spirit becomes in the kingdom, the more critical he will become.

Every decision is questioned.

Each statement, challenged.

From there, comes competition. A fight to win the hearts of the people. His spirit will bring division and dissension, disloyalty and gossip. The Absalom spirit is there, filling his followers minds with criticism and doubt. He has no problem berating the pastor, embarrassing the deacons and condemning the teachers. With the right amount of charm and charisma, he continues to win his followers hearts, even as he plans the demise of his leaders.

Under the spell of the Absalom spirit's false humility and eloquent speech, the church is left to wonder if their leadership can really be trusted.

Unless the Absalom spirit is dealt with when first identified, the conflict he can cause within a body of believers is astounding. Sadly, his spirit will claim many casualties as unity is restored to the Kingdom.

The Absalom spirit can be restored. Though Absalom of the Bible met an untimely and grisly death, this does not have to be the case in our churches.

Are you an Absalom? You don't have to be! Wouldn't laying down your bitterness about the past be easier than carrying it the rest of your life?

I guarantee your impact in the Kingdom will be much great as an adopted child of the King, than as His adversary.

Like a bad tooth or a lame foot
Is reliance on the unfaithful in times of trouble.
Proverbs 25:19 NIV

Jezebel was a powerful, yet wicked queen. We read her story in 1 Kings. She is married to a man named Ahab. Ahab is painted as a passive king with no backbone when it came to his wife.

Jezebel was a Baal-worshipper and false prophetess. Baal was the god of the harvest, god of prosperity, fertility and sex. In this religion, child sacrifices were not uncommon.

Jezebel's spirit can still be found in the world, and in our churches, today. Like Absalom, she was met with an early and gruesome death, but many lives were shattered before that day came. How much more, the spirit of Jezebel continues its path of destruction throughout the Kingdom of God.

One of the stories we read of Jezebel's life involves a man named Naboth. Naboth had a vineyard that Ahab wanted. Being the king, Ahab felt he had a right to it. Naboth said, "thanks, but no thanks." He wasn't interested in selling his inheritance.

Ahab did the expected thing of a grown man – and went home and pouted.

Jezebel found out and took matters into her own hands. When all was said and done, Naboth's reputation had been destroyed, turning his people against him and costing him his life.

This continues to play out in various forms in the western church today.

The Jezebel spirit sees something she wants and will stop at nothing until she has attained it. She gains power by destroying others. They try to situate themselves into places of leadership and it is hard to replace them once there.

She is controlling, domineering and manipulates situations to her liking. The Jezebel spirit can present herself as either an intimidating force or with the sweetness and charm of an innocent child. She chooses what is necessary in the moment to gain what she is after.

Jezebel in the Bible was vicious – and her spirit is the same. She is critical of others and willing to go for the jugular. Children have little to no value to her (remember the child sacrifices?). She sees them as annoying and useless. The Jezebel Spirit loves the spotlight, is never wrong and will draw in others to bring down her victims. When those she recruits choose to no longer play her game, the Jezebel spirit is angered and willing to attack those who were once an alliance.

The Jezebel spirit is a narcissist. She feels nothing about the feelings of others but rather acts the victim in an effort to win people's sympathies. This leaves the real victims – the Naboths, abandoned with no one to ask for help.

While the Jezebel spirit can rest on either men or women, it is more often found with women. She tends to marry an "Ahab" – a husband that is passive and willing to follow her lead. The Jezebel spirit is willing to lie, cheat, steal and attack. If you cross one who holds the Jezebel spirit, you are forever in their cross hairs and, as long as they carry this spirit, they will not forgive you.

Both the Absalom and Jezebel spirits need to be identified and dealt with in the Kingdom. This is an area where spiritual fathers and mothers must remain strong and courageous – not allowing this form of Orphan Spirit bring harm and division among sons and daughters.

Those with the Jezebel spirit are normally unable to recognize it in themselves and it is a difficult spirit to break. Though challenging to deal with, sons and daughters have the authority to cast it out of the Kingdom. Their responsibility is to remain close to the Father, listen only to His voice and purge the Kingdom of all that is not of Him.

CHAPTER 18
THE ULTIMATE FATHER

In our broken world, oftentimes, our view of what a father looks like becomes skewed.

We call God our Father, and that He is. But what kind of Father is He? Let's begin by first considering the responsibilities of a father.

A father's responsibility towards their children is to love, protect, nurture, provide, guide, and validate. Traditionally, the child takes on the name of the father – thereby carrying his identity.

I want to take a look at how, or if, God does these things as well for His children.

My greatest revelation of God's love for me didn't happen until after I became a mother. I remember sitting in our big, burgundy (because burgundy was once cool) recliner, rocking this precious little child. I'd watch Tyler's tiny chest rise and fall with the quick puffs of air that newborns breathe.

His little fingers and toes amazed me – so delicate, intricate and perfect. I knew I would do everything in my power to protect this child.

I've had multiple opportunities to do just that, but there is the one day that stands out in my mind like no other.

We were living in a little house out in the country. By this time, Tyler was three. Since Tim and I were both farm kids, I felt it would be a sin to not have chickens of our own. Tim didn't have the same conviction, but he humored me and soon we had a tiny flock providing more eggs than we needed.

I didn't mind the hens but those roosters were born mean.

I hated those things!

Apparently the feeling was mutual.

From the moment I stepped into that hen house, I never could predict which angle I'd be attacked from. My calves got pecked. My arms got pecked. Even my backside got pecked.

Have I mentioned how much I hated those things?

One day, I was digging in the flowerbeds while Tyler, played in the yard. I heard him shriek in terror and realized he had wandered across the yard near the chicken coop. Somehow, one of the roosters got out and was headed straight for my little boy. The rooster's wings and neck were outstretched and in no time at all, he had attacked Tyler.

Time stood still as instantaneous anger filled my senses. My ears began to ring. My head buzzed. My breathing came out in a low guttural tone as all fear of said rooster left my being.

Conveniently enough, a red plastic bat lay nearby and I swooped in and grabbed it as I raced across the yard towards my baby. No stupid rooster was going to get away with attacking my son!

Feathers flew as I came at the rooster with a vengeance. Blame it on Mama Bear syndrome or a redhead's temper – I don't care. All I knew in that moment was that my son needed me and no matter how many times that rooster had caused me pain, he had only now discovered how to truly unleash my fury.

We all walked away from the fight – the rooster with a sore backside and my promise ringing in his ears that he was about to become chicken soup. My anger was so intense, it felt otherworldly. When I came to my senses, I couldn't help but glance towards the neighbor's home, hoping they hadn't seen the ruckus. I breathed a sigh of relief that their blinds were closed and their car was absent from its normal place in the driveway.

Tyler, who was just starting to talk, couldn't stop reminding me of the incident. "Mama hit da dumb bird. Right? Right, Mama? Mama hit da dumb bird. Right? Right, Mama?"

Though slightly embarrassed at the sight it must have been, I knew I'd do it again in a heartbeat.

Unwilling to allow him further access to my son, I kept my promise to that rooster, and a few weeks later he found himself in a mason jar on our basement shelf. Never had chicken noodle soup tasted so good. I smiled with satisfaction. I had won in the end.

God spoke to me through that incident though, "That's how I feel about you, Lynette. That's how I feel when I see the enemy attacking you."

I couldn't imagine God losing all sense of decorum in His anger of my pain. But then He showed me Psalm 18 . Here's a portion of that chapter:

The cords of death entangled me;
the torrents of destruction overwhelmed me.
The cords of the grave coiled around me;
the snares of death confronted me.
In my distress I called to the Lord;
I cried to my God for help.
From His temple He heard my voice;
my cry came before Him, into His ears.

You ready? Here it comes!

The earth trembled and quaked,
and the foundations of the mountains shook;
they trembled because He was angry.
Smoke rose from His nostrils;
consuming fire came from His mouth,
burning coals blazed out of it.

That sounds like one ticked off Papa!

Smoke billowing from His nose and fire coming from His mouth? Throwing bolts of lighting and hailstone? Yep, He's definitely angry! Suddenly I wasn't quite as embarrassed about my intense passion when it came to protecting Tyler from the attacks of that rooster.

Let's read on...

He parted the heavens and came down;
dark clouds were under His feet.
He mounted the cherubim and flew;
He soared on the wings of the wind.
He made darkness His covering,
His canopy around Him—
the dark rain clouds of the sky.
Out of the brightness of His presence clouds advanced,
with hailstones and bolts of lightning.
The Lord thundered from heaven;
the voice of the Most High resounded.
He shot His arrows and scattered the enemy,
with great bolts of lightning He routed them.
The valleys of the sea were exposed
and the foundations of the earth laid bare at your rebuke, Lord,
at the blast of breath from your nostrils.
He reached down from on high and took hold of me;
He drew me out of deep waters.

Isn't that a beautiful picture?

He rescued me from my powerful enemy,
from my foes, who were too strong for me.
They confronted me in the day of my disaster,
but the Lord was my support.
He brought me out into a spacious place;
He rescued me because He delighted in me.
NIV

Ahhh… peace… the battle is over. He reaches down and takes hold of His child. He takes them out to a spacious place. He rescues His children because He delights in them.

Don't try to tell yourself you aren't loved by your Father God. He is passionate about His children! He gave up His own Son in order to be able to call you and me His own.

The most famous verse in the Bible tells us that "God so loved the world, that He gave His only begotten Son, so that whoever believes on Him will not perish, but will have eternal life." John 3:16 NIV.

He gave His only Son.

For you.

For me.

Like my friends who longed to adopt, God the Father dreamed of bringing us into His Kingdom. He knew there would be a price to pay and He was willing to give up all He had to buy us back.

God has a plan for your life, yes. But so does Satan. John 10:10 reminds us that Satan is looking to steal, kill and destroy, but Jesus came so that we might have an abundant life. When God sees Satan coming at His child, His wrath is stirred. When we call on Him, He is ready and waiting to come to our rescue.

Another, more unpopular, aspect of fatherhood is discipline.

Most parents would agree that this is not an enjoyable necessity, and we are looking at a generation being raised without it, even now.

Do I love disciplining my children? Not even a little. But the truth remains that punishing them isn't about me – it's about them.

A godly parent knows that to raise healthy, productive and happy children, we must give them boundaries. When those lines are crossed, there are consequences. Many parents choose to not follow through with the consequences because it's too hard, too uncomfortable or too painful for the parent.

We'd rather avoid the issue and hope it will go away but, to do this, is to deprive our children of the gift of a parent. We are, in essence, leaving them as orphans. In our well-intentioned desire to bring them joy, we actually handicap our children spiritually and emotionally when choosing to avoid punishment.

God loves us enough to bring discipline into our lives when we push against the parameters He's set out for us. Hebrews 12:5-11(NIV) states,

"My son, do not make light of the Lord's discipline,
and do not lose heart when He rebukes you,
because the Lord disciplines the one He loves,
and He chastens everyone He accepts as His son."
Endure hardship as discipline;
God is treating you as His children.
For what children are not disciplined by their father?
If you are not disciplined—and everyone undergoes discipline—
then you are not legitimate, not true sons and daughters at all.
Moreover, we have all had human fathers who disciplined us

and we respected them for it.
How much more should we submit to the Father of spirits and live!
They disciplined us for a little while as they thought best;
but God disciplines us for our good,
in order that we may share in His holiness.
No discipline seems pleasant at the time, but painful.
Later on, however, it produces a harvest of righteousness and peace
for those who have been trained by it.

As we read earlier, Jonah had to experience God's punishment. God had given him directions but he chose his own and paid for it big time!

When my husband, Tim, was a (super-cute) little boy, he got in trouble one day.

It happened on a Sunday morning in the church parking lot. The service had already ended and while his parents visited with friends inside, Tim found a rock...now he just needed something to throw it at.

He looked around, and there it was – coming down the road. Perfect! A moving target!

As the car approached, Tim hauled off and threw with all his might.

This happened several times until...his dad found out.

Tim was so busted.

To make matters worse, his dad decided to wait until they got home to incorporate Tim's punishment. Tim was sick about it.

Hoping to avoid the inevitable, he became the sweetest, most loving child he could muster up – hoping to change his father's mind.

On the ride home, he sang out, hoping his father would hear him and either forget or relent. But, unfortunately for Tim, "Jesus Loves Me" and "The B.I.B.L.E." didn't bail him out.

As soon as they pulled up to their home, his dad told Tim to meet him in the office (wa…wa…waaaa…)

Isaiah gave a prophecy saying, "these people honor me with their lips, but their hearts are far from me." Jesus repeated those words Himself when talking about the religious.

Tim's story and Isaiah's prophecy have a lesson in them for us today and as much as I would rather give words full of atta-boys and way to gos – I can't.

Why?

Because the rock throwing has to stop.

It just does.

It's no secret that the world is full of crazy! It's easy to feel overwhelmed and discouraged.

I get it.

It's a mess.

But when the words coming from the lips of God's children are like so many rocks in the hands of a little boy, then we have issues.

We need to be a safe place for one another within the walls of the Kingdom – it's time for us as brothers and sisters to stop throwing stones!

At a recent worship service, as the church sang out about how God makes all things work together for our good – I saw it – the Western body of Christ, much like a little boy singing in the back seat on the ride home, hoping their Father will forget or ignore their sin – after all, look at us now – so clean, so happy, so sinless. Please make it all work out for our good... for what we call good.

But you see, Tim wasn't singing his Sunday School songs for God...or even his dad. No, he was singing for himself.

He knew punishment was coming and he hoped his quick fix would reduce or even eliminate his impending punishment.

To worship God in order to gain His approval for our benefit is the exact same thing. And it's idolatry. It is the worship of self.

God isn't looking for worshippers whose only focus is what they, themselves, will gain from their act. That's not true worship!

Either way, God still knows – He knows about the rocks we're throwing at the world (those filthy sinners), He knows about the stones thrown inside the church walls (did you hear what she did? eyeroll) and more than that – a cute outfit isn't enough to hide the emotional affair you're having at work and the neatly pressed shirt and tie aren't enough to hide the secret links you like to pull up on your smart phone... He knows.

And He wants so much better for you.

All the singing....all the good works...all the Sunday morning attitude changes aren't enough.

Is the world a mess?

It is.

But when our lives are just as messy, we have no business going out and condemning others just because their sin is open – and ours remains neatly hidden inside the whole Christian package.

It's time for the church to shut their mouths for a moment and study their hearts. What are your motives? What are your thoughts? Do you hate your sister in the church? Are you justifying a secret sin?

It needs to end!

And after the shutting up...the self-analysis... the repentance is over and we find ourselves fully surrendered in the Presence of God, it is then we can rise up and honor Him with our lips from a pure heart.

People wonder what kind of God would allow pain in the lives of His children? The answer is simple – one that loves them enough to not let them get away with sin. Sin always leads towards pain and loss.

Always.

You can never leave the safety of God's presence and not count the cost...but to return to Him is free – Jesus already paid that price.

Finally, God gives us a place in His Kingdom. He gives us an identity. In 1 John 3 (NIV), it says, *"See what great love the Father has lavished on us, that we should be called children of God! And that is what we are!*

He has made us His children – an heir to His Kingdom.

The Orphan Spirit refuses to acknowledge and accept this free gift, but it stands available, waiting to be accepted.

Are you an Orphan Spirit?

Have you fought your way through, longing for love, yet unwilling to trust? Maybe you've seen yourself at times throughout the stories in this book, I know I have. The purpose of this writing is to invite – no compel us to lay aside our orphan mindset and take on the mind of Christ.

To see God for the Father that He is – the Father that He longs to be in our lives!

To learn to love our Kingdom siblings as He has called us to.

To discover the ways of Kingdom living.

To live free and unhindered as sons and daughters of the King.

CHAPTER 19
THE WAYS OF ROYALTY

Kate Middleton captured our hearts much like her beautiful mother-in-law, Princess Diana, did so many years earlier.

Kate is the closest thing we have to a real-life Cinderella story.

Though wealthy, Kate was raised in an average family. Her ancestors were coal miners and builders. In short, she was born a commoner.

Had she ever dreamt of marrying the prince? Did she even have the right to dream of living in the palace? Perhaps, but the dream would have seemed highly unlikely and only that – a dream.

And then one day, she met him – Prince William, and it wasn't long before they fell in love and made plans to marry. But becoming royalty required a transformation.

She had to learn the ways of royalty. The royal family knows that every aspect of their lives are being watched by the public and every detail is being discussed – whether good or bad. Kate began a rigorous process that groomed her for royal living. She learned how to act, how to walk, how to eat, how to dress, how to speak. She had to learn how to live in a way that brought honor to the kingdom.

On her wedding day, Kate got a new name – Catherine, Princess of Cambridge, and with it came the rights and privileges of being a part of the royal family.

Her experience is an excellent illustration for the Kingdom of God. Once we leave our past life, we take on a new name, a new way of living and a new mindset. It requires transformation.

Romans 12 invites the children of God to be "transformed by the renewing of your minds." To leave our Orphan Spirit behind, means taking on a new spirit – the Holy Spirit. God calls us to a life empowered by His presence in our lives.

This means laying down our boxes of broken dreams, desires, and gifts at the door. God is not a Father without concern for our dreams and desires. Rather, He has dreams and desires for us as well – often dreams that correlate with ours.

1 Corinthians 2 says,

> *"What no eye has seen, what no ear has heard,*
> *and what no human mind has conceived"—*
> *the things God has prepared for those who love Him—*
> *these are the things God has revealed to us by His Spirit.*
> *The Spirit searches all things, even the deep things of God.*
> *For who knows a person's thoughts except*
> *their own spirit within them?*
> *In the same way no one knows the thoughts*
> *of God except the Spirit of God.*

> *What we have received is not the spirit of the world,*
> *but the Spirit who is from God, so that we may*
> *understand what God has freely given us. (NIV)*

Kate Middleton couldn't have imagined her life becoming what it is today – not even in her wildest dreams. Who was she to see herself as one who would be royalty?

The Orphan Spirit sits in the pews of the church and questions the same thing – who am I? What value do I hold?

His fears distort his vision, causing him to see others as a means to an end – a rung on his ladder – an object to control. King Saul was also a commoner who became royalty. The thought overwhelmed him – you can read the story in 1 Samuel 10. When it came time to anoint Saul as king, he hid. Samuel was looking for him and found him hiding among the baggage. Samuel anointed Saul and then wrote the ways of royalty on a scroll explaining the rights and duties of a king.

The Kingdom of God has millions hiding among the baggage of their lives… just like Hadassah. God saw her as Tia, a princess, yet she couldn't see beyond her past.

Like Saul, it's time to rise up out of our hiding places and take our rightful place in the kingdom.

It's time to lay aside our Orphan Spirit and live as sons and daughters of the King!

> *I will not leave you as orphans;*
> *I will come to you.*
> *John 14:18 NIV*

Printed in the United States
By Bookmasters